Insider Guide

Ace Your Interview! The WetFeet Insider Guide to Interviewing

2004 Edition

WetFeet®

Helping you make smarter career decisions.

WetFeet Inc.

609 Mission Street

Suite 400

San Francisco, CA 94105

Phone: (415) 284-7900 or 1-800-926-4JOB

Fax: (415) 284-7910

E-mail: info@wetfeet.com

Website: www.wetfeet.com

Ace Your Interview! The WetFeet Insider Guide to Interviewing

ISBN: 1-58207-369-4

Table of Contents

WetFeet®

Interviewing at a Glance

Demystifying the Interview Process

- Instead of prepping for every conceivable question, concentrate on what you want interviewers to know about your strengths.
- Tell memorable stories to illustrate your strengths.
- Highlight your experience as a valuable team player, not just a solo superstar; your interviewers' top priority is finding coworkers who work well with others.
- Get a job description and read it carefully, so you know exactly what the job entails and how you might shine in the position.
- Try a surefire but oft-overlooked job interview strategy: Show your enthusiasm.

Getting Ready

- Match your strengths, experience, goals, and interests to those of your prospective employer. Look for keyword cues in job postings to get a handle on what the job is really like, and identify your competitive advantages.
- Learn to read between the lines of job postings, so that you can ask smart questions to identify whether this position is a good fit for you and impress your interviewer.
- Bone up on the organization and industry using insider contacts, the company website, trade publications, news reports, and company reports.
- Be prepared for questions about lessons you've learned the hard way, personal interests, career shifts, and long-term goals.
- Line up references that can best attest to your strengths, giving them an explanation of the position and plenty of advance notice.

Basic Interview Expectations

- Make sure your outer appearance reflects the strengths you'll bring to the position.
- Leave them something to remember you by: articles about your work, extra copies of your resume, a portfolio to peruse.

- Control your voice, gestures, and other mannerisms to be sure your body language conveys good things about you.
- To build rapport, seek common ground and show your sense of humor.
- Loosen up and make your Q&A session a pleasant peer-to-peer interaction instead of a lowly-applicant-to-all-powerful-examiner transaction.
- Come in prepared to answer common interview questions, and some tough ones as well.

Interview Types

- The phone screen is actually a first-round interview—so prepare accordingly, with a cheat sheet of examples, anecdotes, and questions.
- Make a good impression on the phone with active listening and a confident tone of voice.
- Sail through online screenings by asking yourself why the employer is asking this question, what the expected answer is, and how you can give an answer that is honest and presents your experience in the best light.
- Job fairs aren't just for students—they're for anyone looking to switch careers or industries or expand their career horizons.
- Get comfortable with different interview approaches, including behavior-based, hypothetical, cases, job simulations, and panel interviews.

Concluding Gracefully

- Show your interest and aptitude with intelligent, informed questions.
- Probe for key information about the position diplomatically, to find out whether this is a job you really want.
- Before you leave, take the opportunity to correct any misstatements, recap your strengths, tell the interviewer you want the job, and ask about next steps.
- Use thank-you notes to reinforce the positive impression you've made and stay top of mind when it's time to make a hiring decision.

Demystifying the Interview Process

- What Employers Want
- How to Give It to Them

WetFeet®

Dating, dancing, walking on fire . . . interviewing has been compared to many activities, and there is some truth to each of these comparisons. Everyone hopes to hit it off with an interviewer and be welcomed into a new workplace like family. At its best interviewing can be quite a tango, where you feel as sharp as you look, give as good as you get on the Q&A, and make impressive career moves with added flair. At its most harrowing, of course, interviewing can leave you feeling raked over the coals, with the flushed cheeks and cold sweat to prove it.

But put the fears, dreams, hopes, and metaphors aside for a moment, and recognize that at its most basic, an interview is simply a conversation about a job. You've had conversations before, right? Then you've already explored ideas with another person, posed thoughtful questions, given considered answers, and kept the conversation rolling until it reached a natural conclusion. Congratulations—you've already got the basic skills needed to succeed in an interview.

Additional preparation is needed for interviews, and of course there is more at stake for both participants—you're talking about a possible career change, not just the possibility of watching the game together on Sunday. This book will help you make the preparations necessary to keep that conversation focused, productive, and pleasant, so that you can keep your wits about you even when the stakes seem alarmingly high. Also sprinkled throughout the book are real-life anecdotes to help you keep the interview recommendations in perspective. No one gets it exactly right all the time, and yet interviewees almost always live to tell the tale—and sometimes land the job, to boot.

If this seems like a lot of extra effort for a half-hour conversation, just think what a difference that conversation can make to you, your career, and your family. And remember, you're not in this alone. Your interviewer probably sat exactly where you are not long ago and is probably concerned about keeping up the other end of the conversation. Ultimately, you and your interviewer are both hoping for the same thing from this conversation: You want it to go well and be the first step toward a productive working relationship.

What Employers Want

The prospect of that worst-case-scenario interview is enough to make even seasoned interviewees break out in a cold sweat. Trick questions. Brainteasers. Panel interrogations. Oh my! But as complicated and convoluted as their interview questions may sometimes seem, all employers really want is to identify a candidate with a demonstrable capacity to deliver results, hire that person, and get back to their other work before it starts to pile up. So give employers what they want and be the candidate they're looking for.

And what about all those esoteric hypothetical scenarios and trick questions? Good news: They're falling out of favor with employers, because they simply aren't that effective. "It used to be that interviewers would ask questions like, 'Tell me three good things about yourself and three bad things' or 'If you were a tree, what kind of tree would you be?'" says William C. Byham, Ph.D., CEO of Development Dimensions International, a human resources research and consulting firm. "Now, they're much more likely to do what's known as behavioral interviewing, where they try to predict your future behavior by asking you for a detailed description of what you've done in the past in particular situations. The good news for candidates is this kind of interview is actually easier to prepare for." (Source: Anne Fisher. Are You Ready for that Big Job Interview? *Fortune*. February 2, 2003.)

So instead of preparing to rack your brains for answers to complicated questions, you should prepare to shine. Know your strengths, and highlight them in anecdotes about previous professional experience. Smarts aren't the only asset that counts with employers—in fact, being a team player is now considered even more important. Make sure that the personal strengths you plan to emphasize in your interview match the demands of the position as indicated by the job description and your background research. (If your strengths are not a strong match for the position, your time would be better spent looking elsewhere for a more suitable position.) Then on the big day, present yourself as a candidate with specialized skills and general-audience appeal. Your confidence, enthusiasm, knowledge, and understanding should confirm what your interviewer is already predisposed to believe: That bringing you in for an interview was a wise move, and that hiring you would be even more brilliant.

When interviewing you, hiring managers are hoping to find the answers to some basic questions—without actually asking those questions. Forewarned is forearmed, so we've broken these questions down for you in the following sections.

Do I Want to Work with You?

Many candidates enter an interview prepared to recite a litany of skills and work experience—but interviewers aren't looking for a walking, talking resume. If you've been invited for an interview, they're already sufficiently intrigued by your skills. The reason they need to meet with you in person is to gauge the personal strengths or competencies you would contribute to the team. Intangible attributes, such as resourcefulness, initiative, creativity, adaptability, drive, and integrity, will set you apart from other qualified candidates.

Know your strengths. Think about which of your personal strengths would be most useful in the position you've applied for, and emphasize these in your interview. Not every one of your personal attributes will be applicable—for example, a tendency to thrive on competition might not be welcome in a small, laid-back office where you'd be the only person in the sales department. But overall, you should find that the personal strengths necessary for this position closely match your own. Otherwise, your time might be more wisely spent finding a job better suited to your strengths than interviewing for a position that goes completely against your grain.

Tell a memorable story. It's critical to provide examples of how your strengths have benefited previous employers. You should have an anecdote ready to illustrate each of your personal strengths in action. Simply telling your interviewers that your attention to detail is impeccable without backing up that statement probably won't convince them. If you really want to impress your interviewers with your attention to detail, tell them about a time when you prevented your company from having to release a new version of a software program by identifying a bug that had gone undetected through two previous rounds of QA (i.e., quality assurance testing). Leave your interviewers with that memorable mental image of you double-checking every aspect of the software, and when it comes time to make a hiring decision, they'll remember your outstanding attention to detail, not to mention the positive impact your strengths had on the company.

Get your stories straight. Unsupported statements about how great you are probably won't sell your interviewers on your strengths, even if that statement comes from a reference. So when you approach your colleagues for references, let them know which examples of your work might be most relevant to your interviewer. Here's how you might prompt a reference: "I'd be in charge of new software development in this position, so they'd probably be interested to hear about that time we were working around the clock on product X, and I came across that bug." If your interviewers hear the same story from two different sources, they're more likely to remember and believe it.

Case in Point: Can I Get a Witness?

Personal references should be, well, personal, since employers are always looking for team members who are both professional and personable. Prompt your references to describe what they've enjoyed about working with you, and they will help you land the job. Consider the following case in point:

"A prospective client once asked me for references as part of the selection process for a website development project I'd bid. I spent some time thinking about the main concerns my prospective client had expressed: that the job get done without being stressful in the process and that the site be inexpensive without looking like corners were cut. So I called some of my repeat clients and asked them to be prepared to describe a typical day working on a website project with me and to describe how much better their sites looked than they'd expected. Before long I got the phone call: 'We want you on the job. We're convinced that you know how to deliver creativity and value—and we want to hear some of these jokes we kept hearing about, too!'"

Will You Mesh with the Team?

According to a 2003 study by the non-profit Level Playing Field Institute, both employees and employers consider "being a team player" to be of paramount importance in the workplace—in fact, respondents found it "more important than doing a good job, being intelligent, being creative, making money for the organization, and many other 'good' qualities in terms of getting ahead in the organization." (Source: Level Playing Field Institute. How Opportunities in the Workplace and Fairness Affect Intergroup Relations Study. www.lpfi.org.) Consider yourself warned: Since "fitting in" is a subjective criterion, it can be much tougher to satisfy than more objective qualifications, like skill sets.

Smarts aren't sufficient. During an interview, you should make an effort not only to impress your prospective employer with your smarts, but also to convey what a thoughtful, pleasant person you are to work with. As social theorist Malcolm Gladwell points out in his influential article "The Talent Myth: Are Smart People Overrated?," employers are learning that intelligence isn't always the most desired attribute for prospective employees, especially when it comes at the expense of teamwork and collective common sense—after all, perfectly smart people were responsible for the debacles at Enron and Arthur Andersen. (Read the article for yourself at www.gladwell.com.)

Although many interviewees still seek to dazzle employers with their individual brilliance, this is a rookie's mistake in a work world that is increasingly dependent on teamwork rather than brainiac star-power. Gladwell quotes Richard Wagner, a psychologist at Florida State University, as saying, "What I.Q. doesn't pick up is effectiveness at common-sense sorts of things, especially working with people. In terms of how we evaluate schooling, everything is about working by yourself. If you work with someone else, it's called cheating. Once you get out in the real world, everything you do involves working with other people." In fact, a research study by Gartner Inc. estimates that "by 2005, knowledge workers will spend nearly 70 percent of their time working collaboratively." (Source: Rebuilding the Competitive Foundation. Gartner Inc.)

Your role on the team. To show prospective employers that you're prepared for the teamwork most jobs now entail, be sure to highlight your experiences as part of a successful team—not just your solo achievements—in your interview. Managers can and should talk about their experience assembling a first-rate team, for example, or the fact that their team surpassed quarterly projections for six consecutive quarters. Specialized employees can emphasize their ability to form effective collaborative partnerships spanning departments or areas of expertise—for example, an editor might talk about working with the IT team to build an effective content management system, or a graphic designer might describe her experience as part of the team responsible for a successful new product launch.

"We" can make all the difference. If your interviewer asks you to describe what you would do in a work scenario, be sure your answer involves teamwork—consulting colleagues, group brainstorming, or making use of expertise in other departments. In other words, your response should not only include an explanation of "what I would do," but also a statement of what "we could accomplish" with a collaborative approach. When you role-play your interview with a friend, note how many times you use the word "we," because your interviewers certainly will.

Case in Point: Impress the *Entire* Team

Don't think that you're a shoo-in for the job just because you've impressed the powers that be. Make it your mission to impress everyone you come into contact with in the interview process. Learn your lesson from this case in point:

"Recently I was interviewing someone for a position on our team who was an inside referral, very well connected to executives in our company. She was plenty smart and enthusiastic, but she must have felt that the job was already in the bag because she came dressed casually, wearing jeans. But what bothered me most of all was that the entire time we talked, she was looking out the window; it was as if she had someplace better to be. With no eye contact, there was no way to establish trust or tell whether she really cared about the job. We couldn't be sure she was really going to be a team player, and that cost her the opportunity."

Do You Really Understand the Job?

Before you head into any job interview, you need to know what you're in for—and that means finding the following information in the job description:

Position title. Many job seekers use titles as search criteria, and don't look twice at positions with unfamiliar titles. But titles can be misleading, so don't be too quick to discount a job based on the title alone. The salary may be better than you expect, and the actual day-to-day responsibilities may be far more varied, interesting, and high-level than indicated by the title, too. So be sure to read over the company information, day-to-day responsibilities, and salary before you decide whether a position sounds promising.

Company information. This may include the name, industry, history, and location of the organization offering the position; use this information as the starting point for your research (see the next chapter). Sometimes the organization's name is not given in the posting. Don't be dismayed—you may be able to figure out the company's name simply by checking the domain name in the contact e-mail address or through an Internet search that cross-references two or more of the organizational specifics provided (e.g., industry and location).

Qualifications. This typically includes years of experience, core competencies or areas of specialization, required skill sets (e.g., software programs, language skills, other technical skills), and degrees or certifications. In addition to required qualifications, a job posting often lists desirable qualifications or skills; if you can demonstrate that you meet these criteria, your application is likely to rise to the top of the heap.

Salary range. Employers do not always provide a salary range, and when they do it is usually listed as "DOE" (i.e., depending on experience). When organizations merely list the salary as "competitive," it's up to you to find out what that means before the interview so that you aren't unprepared when you're asked about your salary expectations. Check salary surveys to find the average salary for the position you are applying for by title, industry, years of experience, and geographic location. (See For Your Reference, at the end of the book, for salary survey sources.)

Benefits. Benefits include vacation, sick/personal leave, sabbaticals, comp/flex time, vision, dental, family/domestic partner insurance coverage, maternity/paternity leave, profit sharing, 401(k) plans, flexible spending accounts, reimbursement for mileage/transportation, per diems, and the like. If a position is described as "non-exempt," that typically means the employee in this position will be entitled to overtime pay or comp time for any hours worked beyond 40 hours per week. Before you accept the position, you should find out whether there are any limits on the amount of comp time or overtime you can accrue. Some employers consider telecommuting a benefit, so if working from home interests you, be sure to ask about that, too.

Responsibilities. This is a crucial part of the job description, since it gives you the best sense of the day-to-day demands and rewards of the job. Too often, candidates focus on the salary offered and on the skills and experience required to land the job, and gloss over the responsibilities they will be required to fulfill. But if you take the time to get familiar with the specific responsibilities of a position, you'll find that you are better able to

- Determine whether the position interests you.
- Match the requirements of the job to your experience and personal strengths.
- Anticipate the interviewer's questions.
- Prepare anecdotes that illustrate relevant strengths and experience.
- Ask informed questions to learn more about the position and the workplace.

Case in Point: Cover Key Benefits

You may not want to bring up benefits until late in the interview process, but be sure you ask about them before you take the job. Sure, you can eventually bargain for a pay raise after you're hired, but it's hard to negotiate better benefits after the fact. Check out benefits and company policies on workman's comp, disability, and maternity, paternity, and elder-care leave even if you don't expect to need them—you never know. Consider the following case in point:

"My current job is one of the best I've ever had, mostly because of my boss. My interview with her lasted 3 hours, mainly because we got to talking about Iowa, where her parents live and where I'm from, and a million other things that had nothing to do with the job. The actual interview lasted about 30 minutes, and the rest was just fun 'girl talk.' The only hitch is that I neglected to ask about the company policy about maternity leave, and in retrospect I wish that I had. I had no idea at the time I was ever going to get pregnant, but it happened not long after I got the job."

Do You Understand Our Business?

Now that you know something about the position and the skills and strengths you need to bring to it, you need to educate yourself on the company's business. In so doing, you will be preparing yourself for success—not just in the interview, but on the job, too. This means research, research, research in each of the following areas. Just how you should go about conducting this research is covered in the next chapter.

Industry. A basic awareness of relevant industry terms and issues is crucial for any interview. This will help you anticipate the questions you'll be asked, speak to the competitive pressures the organization is facing, and ensure that you can understand the terminology your interviewer is using. If you're completely new to an industry, your interviewers will appreciate your effort to learn the ropes and take that as an indication that you're a quick, eager learner. If you've been in the business for years, you'll want demonstrate that you make a point of staying up-to-date on recent developments in your field.

Organization. Researching the organization will help you determine whether this is the right work environment for you, which of your skills and strengths might especially benefit the organization, and what specific organizational challenges you may be able to help solve. This information should give you insight into the organization's culture, needs, and expectations that will help you better prepare for the interview—and not incidentally, give you a key advantage over other candidates for the position. Knowledge is power!

Team. Learn more about the team you'll be working with to gain a better sense of how you can contribute to and advance the team's goals. You'll also need to educate yourself about the team's recent successes. Convey your excitement about the team's accomplishments to your interviewer, and you'll be remembered as an enthusiastic, enterprising candidate who is likely to be an asset to the team.

Last, But Not Least

Once you've done your homework, you may feel you have a solid grasp of the position, industry, organization, and team—but don't think you know it all just yet. In the interview, you should probe for further details and pay close attention to every response your interviewer offers. When the interviewer makes an offhand remark about work styles or team and organizational culture, pay attention and be sure to follow up with a probing question: "I'm intrigued to hear that—can you tell me more?" Nonverbal cues are key, too: If you notice the interviewer make a face or hesitate before speaking, ask follow-up questions on the subject at hand to draw your interviewer out a bit more.

By asking questions, you may discover previously undisclosed demands or rewards of the job. These are critical details that reveal what your interviewer is really looking for in a candidate and ultimately allow you to make an informed decision about whether to accept the job. Your interviewer's hints of a quirky boss and frequent travel could prove problematic or promising, depending on your perspective—but it's far better to discover these details sooner rather than later.

Case in Point: Identify Employer Needs on the Fly

Employers often omit some salient facts about a position from the initial job posting. Sometimes, they just haven't updated the job description in a while; other times, a new project is identified after the ad was posted. Whatever the cause, these undisclosed tidbits can give you a real advantage over the competition. Consider this real-life example:

"When I was interviewing for the job I have now, one of my interviewers mentioned offhand that the company was planning to start using an outside vendor for all graphic design needs, something they had never done before and thus were a little concerned about. I seized the opportunity to explain that I had spent 3 years in a previous position managing the relationship with an outside design agency and that I had intimate knowledge of—and experience avoiding—the potential pitfalls of such an arrangement. I also pointed out that experience in my conversations with subsequent interviewers at the same company, just to be sure that all concerned knew that I had something special to offer. I know that contributed to their decision to hire me."

How to Give It to Them

Once you've learned something about the position and the organization from your research and contacts—plus any hints the interviewer offers—you should have a good sense of which of your strengths to highlight in the interview. Present the right mix of strengths along with generous doses of enthusiasm, confidence, knowledge, and understanding, and employers will be suitably impressed.

Be Enthusiastic

This really is Interviewing 101.

While enthusiasm alone won't land you a job, candidates who fail to convince employers of their enthusiasm can count on being passed over. It's that simple. Why? Because most employers expect an employee's enthusiasm for a job to wane over time. Let's face it: There's some truth to the adage that familiarity breeds contempt. And, if a candidate starts out without much enthusiasm, that doesn't bode well.

When you're preparing for your interview, remember that you'll want to show your strengths, not just tell about them—and enthusiasm is a key strength for any candidate in any position. If you say you're enthusiastic about the position but behave as though you're bored in the interview, what are your interviewers supposed to believe? Your enthusiasm should be clear in your attentive posture, the alert tone of your voice, and a smile that says you are glad to be there. And just so that your interviewer gets the message, be sure to say at the outset something along these lines: "I'm delighted you're taking the time to meet me, because I'm really excited about this position and eager to learn more about it." And, always, always close each interview with a restatement of your interest in the position and enthusiasm about the company.

Focus on Specialty, Hint at Breadth

No doubt you have a wide range of abilities that might impress other people: climbing trees, doing backbends, whistling through your teeth. But unless you're a tree surgeon, a gymnast, or a professional birdwatcher, these are not the abilities you'll want to highlight in a job interview. Stick to talking about talents you know will come in handy on the job you're being considered for, and you'll make a much better impression.

In your interview, present yourself as a specialized professional with general audience appeal. Your interviewer wants to know that you have the specific skills and strengths needed to excel at your job, but also that you are approachable, flexible, and willing to learn. See the Do's and Don'ts table for some rules of thumb to help you achieve the right balance between specialization and general appeal.

Exude Confidence

To inspire an employer's confidence in your abilities, you must demonstrate confidence in yourself. Easier said than done in a nerve-wracking interview situation, but bear in mind the basics of confident body language: Make frequent eye contact with your interviewer, speak up and not too fast, and try to avoid appearing fidgety or overly rigid in your posture.

You'll come prepared to state your strengths and give concrete examples of how you've put them to use, which should inspire confidence in your own abilities. As you state your strengths, neither downplay nor overstate your accomplishments. If you struggle with self-confidence, give yourself a pep talk or, better yet, get an enthusiastic friend or former co-worker to give you one.

If self-deprecating humor or modesty is a habit of yours, role-play with a friend until you can respond to an interviewer's compliments graciously.

Do's and Don'ts for Striking the Right Balance

Don't	Do
Rattle off ten abilities you possess and tell stories demonstrating each. Your interviewer's eyes are sure to glaze over—no one can commit that much data to memory.	Choose three talents to emphasize, and come prepared with three stories about using those talents to help make your point. When it comes to talking up your abilities, less is more memorable.
Focus your comments on a specialty that will only account for a small percentage of your job. If you are applying for a position where your only writing task is the occasional press release, don't spend 10 minutes of your interview talking about what a great writer you are.	Draw a clear connection between your talents and the responsibilities listed in the job description. For example: "I notice the position entails a lot of presentations, client meetings, and conferences, and that suits me just fine—meeting facilitation and public speaking were my favorite parts of my job as a school principal."
Get sidetracked into explaining the technical details of your area of specialization. It could take valuable interview time to explain the subtle differences between the various types of hydroponic tomatoes you were researching at your last job—time that you could (and should) be spending talking about the impact your research had on your former team and organization, and how your research skills might be helpful in the position available.	Consider your audience, and explain your strengths and accomplishments in terms that your interviewer (who may be an HR rep rather than a technical specialist) is likely to understand. Not everyone comprehends the finer points of computer programming, for example, but anyone can understand the cost savings, online sales, and return on investment that can be generated by effective programming. Focus on the problems or opportunities you identified and outcomes you achieved, rather than on processes you used.
Start giving unsolicited advice on how to solve a particular problem you've heard the company is facing. For all you know, the company may have already tried that route or may not be able to afford that solution, and the interviewer may not appreciate the implication that the team lacks the specialized know-how to figure out an effective solution for themselves (even if that's true). Besides, if you give away so much advice for free, why should they bother to hire you?	If asked directly how you would approach a particular problem, ask a few pointed questions that will demonstrate your understanding of the issues involved and then present a couple of pragmatic options that the organization might choose from. Doing so will highlight that you understand that there's more than one "right" way to get the job done.

Do's and Don'ts for Striking the Right Balance (cont'd)

Don't	Do
Say you have no hobbies when you're asked what you do in your spare time. This will lead the interviewer to think of you as less well-rounded and balanced, unwilling to step outside your established area of expertise, and a less than exciting team member. Think about it: Would you want to work with someone who thought of nothing but money all the time, even if that person was an accountant? And remember: Television is not a hobby!	Name a hobby or pastime you truly care about—the reason interviewers ask this question is to witness how passionate you can be. Link your hobby to a personal strength you've developed that may come in handy in this job: maybe knitting taught you how to work patiently and steadily toward your vision, or scuba diving showed you the importance of grace under (water) pressure. If you don't make the link, your interviewer might think of you as an aspiring singer who's just using this job as a way to pay the bills.
Come across as a jack-of-all-trades. If you're equally good at everything, that means you're especially good at . . . nothing. If you've done your homework, you should know which of your strengths are going to interest your interviewer—so don't hesitate to play these up. Even if you've held wildly different jobs in several fields, you should be able to identify a specific area of expertise you've developed that will interest your interviewer. For example, your experience with grant-writing as a social worker and volunteer advocate for your children's school music program could be useful preparation for writing winning client proposals at a graphic design firm.	Be sure you know how to respond to the interview closer that makes most applicants sweat: "Give me three reasons why I should hire you." By the end of the interview, you should have already named all three; this is your opportunity to reiterate those strengths. If your interviewer doesn't ask this question, you may want to recap by summarizing these strengths: e.g., "I'm excited by what we've discussed today. It sounds like my skills in [insert strengths] would be an asset to this position."

An Example

Interviewer: "Your reference couldn't say enough about your fundraising abilities."

Bad response: "Oh, Jim's such a good friend—I guess I'll have to pay him off later!"
A remark like this only undermines the reference and does nothing for you.

Good response: "Thank you. We worked together recently on a fundraising campaign for a local theater, and of course we're both delighted that a new theater program for kids was founded with the funds we raised in that campaign."
This response confirms the interviewer's high opinion of you, and supports that opinion with a concrete example.

Learn to accept compliments from your interviewer graciously.

That said, there's no need to pile on the superlatives with hyperbolic assertions such as, "I am the best you'll find in the business. I can outsell anyone here." This kind of statement inspires the same kind of skepticism as a "World's Greatest Lover" T-shirt: If you're so great, how come your interviewer never heard of you before? Stick to assertions you can support with evidence from your work history. A better assertion would note specifics: "I was the top salesperson at the company for four consecutive quarters."

Demonstrate Knowledge and Understanding

Some interviewees spend the night before their interview boning up on all kinds of trivia about an organization, as though cramming for the test of their lives. But interviews aren't oral exams; they are an exchange between two people, who may soon be co-workers, about shared professional interests. Like any other conversation, an interview requires give and take—so don't expect to dominate it with your own sterling insights about the business; give your interviewer a chance to contribute to the conversation. You do need to know something about the

Case in Point: Know Your Strengths

A job interview is not the time for false modesty. Your references don't chaperone you on interviews, so you need to be prepared to describe your strengths and give examples of how you put them in action. Take a hint from this case in point:

"'How good a writer are you?' the interviewer asked. Not having learned the Art of Elegant Bragging, I said, 'Well, my supervisor said I was one of the three best writers he has ever worked with.' The interviewer replied, 'Yes, but how good a writer do YOU think you are?' My reply was something along the lines of, 'Well, I think I'm very good.' Somehow the tone seemed to change. I didn't get the job. In my job search this year I plan to develop a selection of more powerful statements in response to that question."

industry and the organization, but you're not expected to know it all—just enough to ask your interviewer informed questions, understand the questions your interviewer is asking you, and give a reasonable answer. There will be plenty of time to bring you completely up to speed after you're hired. Meanwhile, your common sense and professional training should prepare you to give sound answers to any questions that may arise about how you would handle a specific problem in the company.

Getting Ready

- Know the Job
- Know the Organization
- Know Yourself
- Line Up Your References

You've just had your morning coffee when you get the call you've been waiting for: Could you come in for an interview next week? You schedule a time, hang up the phone, do a victory dance in your bunny slippers (or boxers) . . . and then what? Hold your breath until the moment of truth next Wednesday? Not if you want to your interview to live up to its promise. Don't wait for the interview to get to work on impressing your interviewers—begin to prepare right now, so that by next Tuesday night you can enjoy the sound sleep of the confident, capable interviewee.

But in every crowd of interviewees, there is one who thinks, "I'm already confident; I can wing it." Maybe that kind of thinking earned you decent grades back in school, but there is no grading curve in an interview. If you're not prepared to shine, chances are someone else will be—and only one of you is going to get the job. Any bets on who that might be? "For any interview, you need to be prepared to show competence and intelligent interest; confidence will only get you so far," says licensed career counselor Rosanne Lurie, author of *Killer Cover Letters and Resumes.* "No interviewer wants to waste time on people who just waltz in with no idea of the organization or industry trends. Their response is, 'If you haven't bothered to take this position seriously, why should I bother to take you seriously?'"

Rather than treating your interview like a performance you can tap-dance your way through, think of it as a jigsaw puzzle that needs solving. You've got strengths, experience, goals, and interests, and your prospective employer does too: How do they match up? Spend some time in advance figuring out exactly why you are the perfect fit for the position, and you won't need any extra fancy steps to land the job.

Know the Job

When you receive that call asking you to interview for the position, the first thing you should do is find the job posting that prompted you to apply for the job in the first place. It's a good idea to make a habit of saving a copy of the job postings you respond to, for just this reason.

You'll want to study the original job posting, because you will be expected to know it cold in your interview. If you don't, you'll come across as uninterested in the position.

Then, dig a little deeper by exploring the keyword cues most job postings offer.

Keyword Cues

Job postings and descriptions contain a host of keyword cues that tell you something about what the employer is offering, the challenges of the position, and the talents and attributes needed to excel. Following are some of the most common keyword cues and what they might mean to you.

Deadline-driven environment

What it really means: A high-stress position.

Give an example of a time when you: Showed grace under pressure, managed a time-sensitive project successfully, and helped your team stay on track for success.

Follow-up questions: Are the major deadlines daily, weekly, quarterly? What kind of project management system do they use to help projects move smoothly?

Detail-oriented

What it really means: May entail juggling tasks that if done incorrectly, could cost the company.

Give an example of a time when you: Identified an opportunity would not otherwise have been pursued, or saved your organization time, resources, or embarrassment by correcting an oversight or finding a more sound solution.

Follow-up questions: What is a typical day like in this position? How much time is devoted to each of the various tasks?

Dynamic/fast-growing company

What it really means: Small, start-up, or floundering company; bosses may be wet behind the ears and disorganized.

Give an example of a time when you: Worked in a company that was going through growing pains and helped your team put effective processes and programs in place.

Follow-up questions: Where do they see the business heading in the next year? Is the funding already secured for the coming year, or is it contingent upon performance?

Earn upwards of $XXX/Earn $$$ at home!

What it really means: This probably isn't a job posting at all, but an ad for a pyramid scheme, a paid training seminar, or an unsalaried commission sales position. Beware!

Give an example of a time when you: Saw a job posting like this and it turned out not to be a job opportunity at all, but rather a paid scheme—then gauge the reaction of your interviewer.

Follow-up questions: Get as much information as you can over the phone before you agree to meet anyone—and if they call it an "opportunity" instead of a position and it sounds too good to be true, think twice about committing your valuable time to an in-person interview.

Fast-paced environment

What it really means: This employer may set unrealistic deadlines and expect you to work your tail off to meet them.

Give an example of a time when you: Were able to turn around a project that exceeded expectations given a very aggressive deadline.

Follow-up question: Ask whether there are project management tools or applications you should learn that would help to keep multiple projects on track—your interviewer will be impressed by your initiative.

Great benefits

What it really means: Pay is probably not great.

Give an example of a time when you: Took a job on a temp-to-perm or trial basis for 3 months so your employer could see your value to the organization before committing to a higher salary.

Follow-up questions: Inquire specifically about what benefits are offered. Be careful, though—you don't want to give hints about any medical conditions that may give your interviewer cause to write you off as a candidate due to the insurance burden (it's illegal for them to ask about medical conditions).

Hands-on position

What it really means: Expect to do a fair amount of grunt work and have the buck passed to you. You probably won't have access to support staff, either.

Give an example of a time when you: Took the initiative to work start-to-finish on a project that turned out to be a real asset to your organization.

Follow-up questions: If it sounds like they're asking for more than any one person can reasonably do, ask whether they're planning to expand the department/that area of their operations in the next year or two. If they say no, think twice about the position—you don't want to be set up for failure.

Highly motivated/dedicated

What it really means: Beware of burnout in this job.

Give an example of a time when you: Went above and beyond the call of duty at a previous job.

Follow-up questions: Ask about how this position became available. If the last person on the job left because of burnout, proceed with caution.

Multi-tasking skills required

What it really means: Multiple bosses and/or constant interruptions in your work may make it hard to get through your workload.

Give an example of a time when you: Were patient and unflappable in juggling responsibilities, without being a total pushover about taking on new ones.

Follow-up questions: Be sure to ask who you'd be reporting to, how many different departments you'd be working with, and how they'd describe a typical day on the job.

PT-perm

What it really means: Either you're going to be expected to prove yourself, or they don't yet have funding for a position that really ought to be full time. Either way, expect to work very hard.

Give an example of a time when you: Took a PT-perm position and were later offered a full-time position because of your excellent performance.

Follow-up questions: If you're interested in full-time work, ask when they expect the position to go full time. If you really only want to work part-time, make that clear up front and suggest that they'll be surprised by what you can accomplish in a part-time capacity. They might be relieved to hear it if they really can't afford you full time.

Pay negotiable

What it really means: Be prepared to negotiate! You will probably be asked to name your salary, so do your salary research (see below).

Give an example of a time when you: Got a raise after a short time, because you were such a valuable asset.

Follow-up question: Besides salary, are there bonuses or commissions for outstanding work?

Room for advancement

What it really means: Either the employer knows this job is thankless and offers little enticements on its own merits, or the organization is committed to promoting employees from within.

Give an example of a time when you: Started at the bottom and rose through the ranks to a position of responsibility.

Follow-up question: What have people who previously held this position gone on to do?

Salary DOE/competitive

What it really means: Salary is yet to be determined, or possibly below industry average for this position.

Give an example of a time when you: Saved or earned money for your organization.

Follow-up questions: Ask if they have a sense of the salary range for the position. From your research, you should know how that corresponds to industry-standard salary ranges.

Self-starter

What it really means: Supervisors are overworked and have no time to oversee you.

Give an example of a time when you: Enjoyed taking the initiative on a project and produced excellent results for the organization.

Follow-up question: Would your supervisor prefer regular reports or meetings about work progress, so that it doesn't interrupt daily workflow?

Team player

What it really means: This could mean one of two very different things. Either you'll be expected to work well collaboratively, or you'll be expected not to complain when your superiors and colleagues have you do some of their spillover work in addition to the job you were actually hired to do.

Give an example of a time when you: Worked collaboratively with a team to complete a project on an aggressive timeline, with excellent results.

Follow-up questions: Ask who would make up your "team" at work. If it will be mostly other people in positions at your same level, give an anecdote of a time when you and your colleagues pulled together to get a daunting project done well. If the other team members are all your superiors and you are the sole underling, ask for clarity on who will be managing your work assignments—you don't want to be responsible for spillover from five supervisors.

Key Tasks

Since many newspapers and career sites charge for classified ads by the word or limit the space available for employment listings, job postings are often a little short on detail about specific tasks you'd be expected to perform. If the job posting does not spell out the specific day-to-day responsibilities for the position, send an e-mail or make a phone call to the employer requesting a detailed job description. This can be a competitive advantage in the interview process: Armed with more details about the position in advance of the interview, you'll have a better sense of what to say and ask than other candidates who didn't bother to inquire about the details.

Consider the example on the following page.

Sample Job Posting

Head Office Manager (FT)

Fortune 1000 company with 30-year track record of growth seeks accomplished professional with 8+ years of office management experience to manage daily operations of headquarters in Chicago. As Head Office Manager, you will have autonomy to make decisions, but also the support staff and resources needed to advance company goals with utmost efficiency and excellence.

Requirements:

- 10–15 years of experience in administrative roles, with at least 8 years in increasingly responsible office management position(s)
- Proven experience effectively interacting with all levels of employees
- Budgeting and fiscal management capabilities
- Expertise in managing a wide range of vendors
- Proficiency with Microsoft project management utilities
- Meeting planning background a plus
- Consumer packaged goods background an asset

Candidates should be prepared to provide at least three professional references attesting to candidate's professionalism, sense of humor, multi-tasking capacity, and excellent people skills.

Salary: above industry standard, DOE

Full benefits package includes excellent health, vision and dental coverage for employee and family; profit-sharing after 1 year; 401(k) with employer matching contributions; flexible spending account; charitable donation matching program.

All resume submissions will be handled with utmost confidentiality. Please indicate source of listing in header.

This posting offers enticing details about the position and the company to encourage job seekers to respond and lists required skills to narrow the number of respondents to qualified candidates. But what does this posting really tell you about the job? You might deduce that there is a fair amount of interpersonal interaction, budget management, staff management, project management, and some meeting planning involved—but that leaves a lot of room for interpretation. This posting leaves you with a lot of questions, namely:

1. What tasks will consume most of your time?
2. Who will you interact with most on a day-to-day basis?
3. Who else will be on your team?
4. How many people will you be expected to manage?
5. Will you be able to set your own budget?
6. Who will you report to?
7. What kinds of vendors will you have to manage?
8. How much will you need to learn about consumer packaged goods to do your job effectively?
9. How many different tasks will you be expected to juggle at any one time?
10. What hours will you work each week?
11. Will you ever have to work weekends or evenings?
12. Is telecommuting a possibility?
13. Is there any specialized knowledge that would benefit you in this job?

Now let's take a look at a detailed job description for the same position:

Sample Job Description

Read over this sample job description carefully, and then see how many of the questions raised by the sample job posting you can now answer. Answers appear on pages 36 and 37.

Title: Head Office Manager

Location: HQ

Status: FT (exempt)
Responsibilities include:

Administrative staff management (40%)

Manage & mentor administrative staff, including front desk, meeting planners, mailroom, and other support staff

Set quarterly goals for administrative staff, and make regular progress reports to VP HR on success toward these goals

Manage office calendar and administrative staff workflow using Microsoft utilities

Assist HR in hiring administrative staff

Facilities management (35%)

Research, budget, and implement all major office-related purchasing decisions, from vendor/supplier selection through final implementation/installation

Oversee support staff and vendors responsible for facilities management, including equipment maintenance

Direct office renovations and ensure ADA and ergonomic compliance throughout office

Sample Job Description (cont'd)

Maintain central calendar for use/availability of HQ facilities

Create and manage office supply budget

Be accessible by beeper for facilities emergencies as needed

Meeting/event planning (25%)

Work directly with Senior Partners to plan major meetings, office events, parties, and trainings

Hire and manage outside vendors (catering, entertainment, etc.) for all HQ events, including Chicago-based trainings, product launches, and conferences with other company divisions

Coordinate off-site receptions, dinners, and entertainment for affiliates as needed by senior management

Be on-call during events and launches in case of emergency

Answers

1. What tasks will consume most of your time?

   Administrative staff management (40%)

2. Who will you interact with most on a day-to-day basis?

   Administrative staff (see above)

3. Who else will be on your team?

   Front desk, meeting planners, mailroom, and other support staff, plus vendors

4. How many people will you be expected to manage?

   At least four staff members (one receptionist, two meeting planners, one mailroom clerk) plus unspecified additional support staff and vendors

5. Will you be able to set your own budget?

   Yes, with approval of superiors

6. Who will you report to?

   HR plus senior partners

7. What kinds of vendors will you have to manage?

   Caterers, party planners, facilities managers, and maintenance

8. How much will you need to learn about consumer packaged goods to do your job effectively?

   Need to know about successful CPG product launch events

9. How many different tasks will you be expected to juggle at any one time?

    Three distinct areas of responsibility, with 14 specific tasks

10. What hours will you work each week?

    Hours will vary; expect to be on call occasionally after office hours

11. Will you ever have to work weekends or evenings?

    Yes

12. Is telecommuting a possibility?

    Flexible schedule may be possible, but given responsibility for administrative staff oversight, seems unlikely

13. Is there any specialized knowledge that would benefit you in this job?

    Product launches, ADA compliance, project and calendar management software

Got most of them correct, did you? Congratulations: You've learned to read between the lines, which will be a useful asset to help you ask informed, intelligent questions on the big day. The information gleaned from the job description will also help you make a convincing case for yourself as the ideal candidate.

Know the Organization

In the course of your job search and networking process, you should have become fairly familiar with the organization where you've applied. But don't stop there—keep asking friends and colleagues what they know about the organization, team or department, and key competitors. Bone up on the organization through industry publications and Web searches as recommended in the sections that follow until you can check off every item on the list below.

And, if you've forgotten why you need to know all this, revisit the first chapter. Look to the last chapter of this Insider Guide to find a number of resources you can use in your research.

☑ Checklist: Background Research

Make a copy of this checklist for each position you interview for.

Industry

- ☐ I am aware of three key competitive pressures facing the industry today.
- ☐ I can think of three competitive opportunities that make this a promising business to be in.
- ☐ I can name the top ten news items in the industry for the past year.
- ☐ When I read through a trade publication, I do not come across many terms with which I am unfamiliar.

Organization

- ☐ I know the company's website very well.
- ☐ I am familiar with this organization's business model and know how it makes its money.

Checklist: Background Research (cont'd)

- ❑ I am aware of the key competitive pressures facing the organization today.
- ❑ I have visited the websites of the organization's three main competitors.
- ❑ I am able to name the company's three main competitive advantages.
- ❑ I can name three of the company's main accomplishments in its history and three major accomplishments in the past year.
- ❑ I can name the top three news items about this company in the past year.
- ❑ I can recount the basics of the company's history, including how the company was founded.
- ❑ I know the names of the top executives in the company.
- ❑ When I read through the organization's website, I do not stumble over any terms.

Team

- ❑ I know the names of the team leaders, including those who would be my direct supervisors.
- ❑ I have read all available team member bios on the website, and know where they are from and what their qualifications are.

The Industry

Be sure to familiarize yourself with relevant industry terms and issues. Read respected industry publications, and do an online search to identify the biggest news stories within the field in the past year. Use this information to ensure that you can speak to the competitive pressures the organization is facing and that you can understand the terminology your interviewer is using. Even if you've been in the business for years, reading a few articles discussing new approaches to common problems is good preparation for any topical questions.

You can find a host of invaluable career- and industry-specific information in the Career and Industry Profiles on www.wetfeet.com. WetFeet also publishes Insider Guides on a number of industries; see the last page of this guide for a list of WetFeet publications.

The Organization

Naturally, you'll first look for information about the company online (check out the many Company Profiles available on www.wetfeet.com), but don't stop there: Send an e-mail to friends and former colleagues to find out whether any know someone who works there or might have a contact there. Explain that you're applying for a position at the organization and would like to get the inside scoop on what it's like to work there. Once you have a contact at the organization, introduce yourself, explain your interest in the organization, and find out whether they're willing to answer some questions. If they are, this conversation could take place over e-mail or the telephone. Refer to the previous checklist to be sure you get as much inside information as you can.

The Team

If you do talk to a contact inside the organization, be sure to ask what that contact knows about the team and the person who will be interviewing you. (You did ask for a name when you received the call asking you to come in for an interview, right? We thought so.) Also, look on the "About Us" page on the organization's website and find out everything you can about the skills and background of everyone on the team, especially the person who is scheduled to interview you. If you can find a point of connection with your interviewer—whether that's a colleague or vendor you both know, a conference you both attended, a different city or country where you both lived—you will both be much more at ease in the interview, and it'll go that much better. Check out the organization's annual report and scan press reports online to find out what the department has accomplished in the last year.

Awards and Accolades

If you've been invited for an interview, clearly they think highly of you. You should be sure to return the compliment by learning about the organization and why it would be a great place to work. Most business magazines produce an annual list of the best places to work, so check out these lists to see whether your prospective employer merits a place. Non-profit organizations and think tanks also offer awards to organizations that have made a positive impact on the community or that have set the standard for best practices in their industry. Think about what's important to you in a company, and the odds are there's an index that tracks the best organizations in that area. Consider the following indexes:

- 50 Most Desirable MBA Employers (www.fortune.com/fortune/mba)
- 100 Fastest-Growing Companies (www.fortune.com)
- America's Best Companies for Minorities (www.fortune.com)

- America's Most Admired Companies (www.fortune.com)
- Best 100 Companies to Work For (www.fortune.com)
- DiversityInc Top 50 (www.diversityinc.com)
- Business Ethics Awards (www.business-ethics.com)
- GreenBiz Leaders (www.greenbizleaders.com/)

To find out whether a prospective employer has garnered any other accolades, do a keyword search on the company's website for "award" or scan the press releases in the press/media section of the site.

Know Yourself

Once you've carefully gleaned every last bit of information from the job description and completed your research on the organization and its industry, you're ready to write your own story. Your resume says a lot about your career, but it doesn't tell the whole story of what you have to offer your prospective employer. That story isn't about places worked, tasks performed, and education received, but a much more exciting tale of strengths discovered, lessons learned, interests pursued, and plans hatched. This is the kind of story that will really engage your interviewer—so start piecing your story together.

Strengths

Many job applicants confuse strengths with skills. Skills are abilities that can be cultivated with a certain amount of training, such as facility with a software application. Strengths are personal attributes that you may have been born with and cultivated over the course of many years and life experiences—perseverance in the face of adversity, for example, or a natural friendliness that makes meeting new people easy for you.

If you lack skill with a certain software program, you may be able to learn it in a few months—but a personal strength is not so easily acquired in a 6-month training course. As a result, interviewers are usually much more interested in candidates who have all the strengths needed to do the job well than in interviewees who can only bring skills to the table, even if some of those skills look mighty impressive on paper. Just think about it: Your fluency in Hawaiian may occasionally come in handy in that administrative position you've applied for, but your impeccable sense of organization will probably be a lot more useful on a daily basis.

"More and more, candidates are evaluated for competencies like initiative, integrity, ability to adapt to change, and valuing diversity," confirms William C. Byham, Ph.D., CEO of the research and consulting firm Development Dimensions International. "Companies also are far more interested than they used to be in trying to figure out an applicant's motivation. . . . For instance, a person who thrives on personal recognition might not be a good fit for a job that requires intense participation in a team." (Source: Anne Fisher. Are You Ready for that Big Job Interview? *Fortune*. February 2, 2003.)

So instead of racking your brain to come up with a long list of skills you have to offer, spend an hour or two on the following exercise:

1. Looking over the job description, make a list of the personal strengths that will probably be required for this job. Is this a position that requires handling large sums of money? Then the right candidate will be someone who's responsible, reliable, and ethical. If it's a customer care position, they'll be looking for someone who is personable, patient, and empathetic.

2. Ponder what personal strengths could be considered a plus for the job, and list those too. If the job description includes budget management, a thrifty nature could be a competitive advantage for a candidate. If it looks like you'll be working with customers overseas, your comfort with other cultures is a definite bonus.

3. For each of the necessary personal strengths for this position, think of an anecdote that illustrates your strength in this regard. Let's say you can recall a time when you caught an oversight on the annual report, and from then on were entrusted with double-checking the financial numbers on all investor communications. That anecdote would help show you're thorough and responsible enough to handle fiscal responsibilities. Or perhaps there was a time a customer was so touched that you'd remembered to ask after his

sick cat Snickerdoodle that he always asked to speak to you specifically and became a loyal customer to your company. Right there you've demonstrated your capacity for empathy *and* the advantage your employer stands to gain from it.

4. Look over your list of personal strengths that might prove helpful in this job, and identify those you possess. Can you think of a story that demonstrates each of these personal strengths? Maybe your thriftiness led you to track down a reliable small accounting firm in Virginia to handle an audit, instead of going with that expensive Big Four firm that was later charged with fraudulent accounting methods. Or perhaps your graciousness as a host for visiting clients from Taiwan helped slowly strengthen that client relationship until your company was brokering most of their business dealings in the United States.

Case in Point: Perfectionists Only Need Apply

If you're not sure of the personal skills your prospective employer is seeking in an employee, take another look at the job description, and consider what you know of the working environment. If you've applied for a high-volume sales job in a fast-moving company, you might expect that grace under pressure and results orientation might come in handy. And if you're applying for an editorial position in an academic institution, you might want to take your cue from the following case in point:

"Once an interviewer asked me, 'Are you a perfectionist? I mean the kind of person who will contemplate the perfect usage of a comma for hours?' And I said, 'Well, no, I can't say that I am that obsessive about punctuation, really,' and then he just got up and walked out of the room, as if I'd just insulted him."

Lessons Learned

Nothing is more suspicious or less impressive than a flawless candidate. Either you're hiding some truly terrible flaw that will become apparent after you've been hired or your abilities have come so easily to you that you have no idea what it's like to really work at developing a skill. Show that you've already learned a few important life lessons, and you'll sound more experienced, wise, hard-working, and human. Hiring managers want candidates who have demonstrated an ability to learn and recover from mistakes. After all, mistakes are inevitable. What's crucial is the ability to bounce back and not repeat the same mistakes.

It's an interviewer's job to probe for possible shortcomings, and many won't quit until you 'fess up to some weakness—so you'd be wise to have a "lesson learned" story ready as an answer rather than admitting a character flaw under duress. But how do you tell a story about making a mistake without losing your credibility, or leading your interviewer to wonder whether you'll make the same mistake again? Here are four key tips:

Beware of TMI (too much information) syndrome. Such stories may be standard fare on reality TV shows, but does your prospective employer really want to know about how you learned the hard way not to date your coworkers or the dangers of cocktails before board meetings? Save these stories for friends or an episode of "Life's Most Embarrassing Moments"—they'll only make your interviewer worry about your judgment, not to mention possible sexual harassment lawsuits and drinking problems.

Keep it work-related. You may have learned a lot when your grandmother passed away recently, but do you really want your interviewer to remember you as the person whose grandmother died? It would be much better to tell the story to a financial planning firm of how you discovered how much more you enjoyed the client problem-solving aspects of website design than the actual coding. Then you'll be remembered as the multi-talented applicant who'd be a natural at helping clients find workable solutions.

Make your interviewer your ally. If you're in the same line of work as your interviewer, chances are your interviewer has experienced some of the same trials you have and will appreciate your graceful handling of a familiar situation. Let's say you're both in the movie business, and in your first production assistant gig you made the mistake of putting your cell phone number on a poster for an open casting call. This story will probably win you a sympathetic groan from your interviewer, who will appreciate the predicament of being flooded with calls from aspiring actors. Then describe a lesson you learned from it that will help you out at the job you're interviewing for—maybe this was the crash course you needed in movie-making protocol or maybe it taught you to be gracious and understanding even when you're inundated.

Explain how the lesson learned relates to this position. If you say you learned that you really don't like elephants and the job you're applying for is in carpentry, that story seems like a bizarre non sequitur. But if you learned that you didn't like working with elephants as much as you enjoyed building sets at the circus, this may actually be a helpful story to get you the job. In other words, be sure that lesson learned is relevant to the position you're interviewing for.

Interests

"I've always found insurance billing so fascinating. . . ."

Hold it right there! Before you make a bogus blanket statement of interest like this in the hopes of pleasing your interviewer, be aware that such a claim might actually sow the seeds of doubt in the mind of your interviewer. This statement is far too broad—which of the many and varied tasks of insurance billing are fascinating, exactly? It's also easily refuted: If you've always known you wanted to enter the field, why did you go to school for interpretive dance instead of getting your certification in insurance billing? You also risk sounding naïve and dreamy-eyed—your interviewer is looking for a candidate who knows the challenges ahead and is prepared to take them on, not someone who is going to quit in disillusioned disgust upon discovering that insurance billing is not in fact endlessly fascinating.

So before you enter your job interview, think carefully about what interested you in the job, and how it ties into other long-standing interests of yours. Which of your interests does insurance billing satisfy? Do you enjoy puzzling through mathematical problems or take particular satisfaction in reconciling discrepancies? Your interviewer is looking to hire someone who is going to be passionate enough about the work to stick with it even when it gets challenging or—worse yet—tedious, rather than someone who wants the job just because it pays well, has reasonable hours, or offers a flexible schedule. What happens when you don't get that bonus or you have to work late to finish a project? Employers are looking for the person who has a long-term interest in the job beyond short-term practical considerations.

Making the leap: advice for career changers. If you are trying to switch careers, a persuasive explanation of your interests can help you make a convincing case for the change. Let's say you're trying to make the leap from a career as a museum curator to a position with a consulting firm that specializes in educational policy. You might begin to build a case based on your interests by answering the following questions:

1. **Why does the position interest you?** As an advocate for the arts and a parent, you've long been concerned that public schools are not providing kids with sufficient opportunities to think creatively and discover their passions. This position is just the opportunity you've been looking for to have an impact on educational policy at a broad level.

2. **What evidence do you have of your interests?** You developed programs for school groups at the museum, served on the board of your state's arts council, and testified at state hearings about the impact of cuts on school arts programs.

3. **How are your interests relevant to the position?** Lobbyists often hire the firm to help them build an effective case for funding school programs, and due to your long-standing commitment to the issue, you'd be both thorough and passionate in mounting campaigns and developing winning grant proposals. Since you've given testimony yourself in state hearings, you can also help coach clients on becoming effective advocates for their programs.

Case in Point: Go with What You Know

Don't exaggerate your skills so that you'll be sweating bullets your first day on the job! Emphasize your personal strengths and relevant experience, and you may land the job as the candidate with the most potential, even if your skills don't exactly match those the employer had in mind. If you don't get the job but make a positive impression on your interviewer with your personal strengths and experience, you'll be first on the list of people to contact when an appropriate position does become available. You never know where a good connection may lead, as this case in point shows:

"I once had an employer tell me 'If we could use your set of skills, I'd hire you in a minute, but we currently don't have need of them. However, I happen to know a guy over at this company who is looking for someone with your skills, and I will recommend you to him, and give you his number to call.' That led to a job for me."

Goals

Once you know how the position matches your strengths, experience, and interests, you need to determine how it contributes to your long-term goals. Even if you're detail-oriented and resourceful and have a demonstrable interest in legal research, that doesn't necessarily mean you're destined to be a paralegal. Maybe you should go to law school instead or become a legal librarian. You need to be clear about how being a paralegal fits in with your life plan—for your own sake and to present a convincing case for giving you the job.

Your interviewer will want assurance that you chose to pursue this job above all other options, rather than simply by default. Perhaps you can convince your interviewer that your goal is to be a paralegal without being entirely sure yourself, but what happens after you get the job and realize that you'd be much closer to your career goal of being a head legal librarian if you'd taken that job in library science instead? Spend some time considering your career path before your interview, and you'll save yourself a lot of backtracking.

You're not just it for the money. When you're considering your career goals, think beyond cold cash. As *Fortune* magazine columnist Noshua Watson points out, a steadily rising salary is not a very meaningful goal, nor is it very realistic anymore: "A 30-year-old today is 50% more likely to have a bachelor's degree than his counterpart in 1974 and earns $5,000 more a year, adjusted for inflation," he says. "But that's where the good news stops. He also has more in student loans and credit card debt, is less likely to own a home, and is just as likely to be unemployed. His salary probably topped out during the boom, whereas his predecessor's rose throughout his career." (Source: *Fortune*, October 14, 2002.) High-paying jobs are also very elusive and extremely volatile, and even successful careers in highly paid fields (such as sports) are often short-lived.

Long-term planning. Even though the "Where do you see yourself in 5 (or 10 or 15) years?" question is not as ubiquitous as it once was, many interviewers continue to cling to it, so you should be prepared with an answer. Interviewers who use this question are trying to gauge some combination of the following: your level of interest in the field or industry you're pursuing, your commitment to the company, and your long-range planning skills.

This can be a very difficult question to answer for those just starting out. Consider the skills that you might develop in the position you're interviewing for, and highlight those in your answer. If you're interviewing for an entry-level position, it's a good idea to figure out what the next two positions in the hierarchy are and mention that, after mastering the position you're interviewing for, you hope to be promoted into one of those.

If you're a midcareer candidate, focus your answer on potential career development areas, such as honing your management skills, or learning more about an aspect of your career that you've yet to explore. It's a good idea to find out about possible career paths in the company you're interviewing with—you don't want to suggest that you'd eventually like to work in the operations department if the company doesn't even have one.

If you're having trouble coming up with a good response, take some time to consider the following goals and related questions:

1. **Impact:** Will this job offer an opportunity for you to change your community, industry, or the world for the better?
2. **Pride:** Does the job description reflect your aptitudes, strengths, and interests?
3. **Achievements:** What opportunities will you have to shine in this job?
4. **Learning:** What subjects will you have an opportunity to explore in this job?

If you can't answer all of these questions, don't worry—the full rewards of a position may not be immediately clear to you until you've been on the job awhile. But if you can't think of any career goals this position will help you attain, there's a problem. Maybe this isn't the right job for you, or maybe your career goals are inconsistent or contradictory. If you want to have lots of adventures on the high seas, then working on a farm may not be the best career move—and you may have to give up on the idea that you can be a sailor all your life and win the Nobel Peace Prize to boot.

If you get the impression from your interview that the position is not going to be as promising for your career as you'd hoped, you should think twice before accepting the position. Ideally, both you and your interviewer should leave the interview convinced that this job is not just another job for you, but rather a sound career move.

Case in Point: Nice People, Wrong Job

They loved you, they called you in for four interviews, they took you out to lunch . . . and they hired someone else. These things happen in the selection process. But the more you interview, the more you learn to not take employment decisions as comments on your character and to regard any meaningful personal contact you've managed to make in an impersonal process as a triumph. Any positive contact in an interview may help you later on and can really boost your professional confidence, as this case in point illustrates:

"I recently found a letter I received from the head of a museum after I'd interviewed with her for a position there. That was one of the better interviews I had, and I got along so well with all the personnel that I met at the museum, but the position I was applying for, as I recall, wasn't a great match for my skills. It says, 'Thank you for going through the whole, long interview process. It was a pleasure getting to know you better. You're a wonderful person and a strong candidate. . . . I'm sure your job hunt will go well, with your skills, background, and winning ways, the perfect match between person and position. I wish you all the best.' I kept the letter because it's so sweet."

Line Up Your References

Many people dread approaching their colleagues and former bosses for job references because they feel like they're asking for special favors or fishing for compliments—but it's all a matter of what you ask. If you were to say, "Robert, I need you to vouch for me with this company where I'm trying to get a job," it might sound a bit presumptuous. You're asking him to put his good name on the line for you, but since you didn't tell him anything about the position, he has no way of knowing whether you're actually a good fit for the position. Don't put your references in an awkward position by demanding their blind faith in you—they might be willing to do it once, but they probably won't want to repeat the experience. Keep your request limited and specific instead, and your references will be much happier to oblige.

Give Advance Notice

When your interviewer calls to set up an interview, don't wait until you're asked to gather references. The right time to ask your colleagues for a reference is not when they're smack in the middle of a project, and you have to interrupt because you've promised to get references to your interviewer tomorrow. If you're calling or dropping in, the first thing you should ask is not "Could you give me a reference?" but "Is now a good time to talk?" You should always approach four or five people who have had substantial experience working with you, in case one or more is inaccessible.

Explain Your Plans

Send an e-mail to each possible reference explaining the opportunity, what you have to offer, and the abilities you'd like them to attest to. Since you know exactly why you want to pursue this job and how it matches your strengths and interests, it should be easy for you to explain your interest and qualifications to potential references. This is good practice for making your case to your interviewer!

There's always a chance that a person you contact won't feel comfortable providing a reference—maybe a current teammate is afraid that giving you a reference would be perceived as encouraging you to leave the company, or someone you worked with in a different industry doesn't feel able to speak to your abilities in another field. Don't put anyone on the spot—a grudging reference is worse than no reference at all. Instead, pose your request as an open-ended question, preferably in an e-mail, along the following lines:

"I've applied for a position as ________________ at ___________________, and I'm really excited about this opportunity, which will put my abilities in _____________________ to good use doing _____________________. This would be an ideal chance for me to pursue my interest in ___________________, so I'm delighted that I've been invited in for an interview. Since we've worked together on projects that require similar _______________________ as this job, would you be willing to provide a reference attesting to my abilities in this regard? Obviously I'd like a strong reference to support my application, so please think it over and let me know if this is something you'd feel comfortable doing.

If you could get back to me with an answer by [date], that would be ideal. I'll send further details about the position and my qualifications. I really appreciate your thoughtful consideration, since this would be a big career move for me."

Supply Three Points

Once you've made the initial approach and scored a few yeses from prospective references, the next step is to make it as easy as possible for your references to give glowing recommendations by providing talking points about the position and the three main strengths that make you an ideal candidate. If you haven't worked with your references in a while, you might remind them of projects that you worked on together that illustrate your strongest qualifications for the position.

Assure your references that this would only entail a phone call and that you'd be most grateful for their time and support.

Follow Up

If, after the interview, you decide that you're not interested in the position, let your references know that they won't be contacted after all and explain why. They'll appreciate your taking the time to keep them in the loop. Likewise, if in the course of interviewing, you discover that your potential employer is concerned about a specific skill or strength that isn't evident from your resume, take the opportunity to let your references know that any positive comments they can offer in that direction will be most helpful.

If you hear that your references were contacted, send them a nice thank-you card—and if you get the job, you might consider sending them a small gift as a token of your appreciation. Everyone likes to feel appreciated, and a reference that is enthusiastic enough to help land you a job deserves tremendous gratitude—and not incidentally, a little added encouragement to keep the praise coming for future jobs.

Even if you find out that they weren't contacted, thank them for their willingness to help and let them know that they're off the hook—for now.

With your research in place, your references lined up, and a strong sense of why you are the ideal candidate for the position, the hardest part of your interview prep is now over. In fact, you're probably raring to go to that interview—but first, look over the next chapter and be sure you've got all the basics covered.

Basic Interview Expectations

- Look the Part
- Bring the Right Stuff
- Make an Entrance
- Say It with Body Language
- Build Rapport
- Master the Art of Q&A

Think of a job interview as a formal social event, like a wedding or company holiday party, where certain social graces, attire, and other trappings are expected. You don't necessarily need to obey all these conventions, but you should know what they are so you can make an informed choice about whether to observe them. There's always a balance to be struck in an interview: You don't want to unintentionally do, wear, or say something that will make you *persona non grata*, but you also want to be sure the way you present yourself is an image you can live with after you get the job.

Look the Part

Most job applicants spend hours tailoring their resumes and crafting cover letters to make sure they put their best foot forward with employers. Yet so many otherwise first-impression-savvy candidates get dressed in a 15-minute mad dash before an interview. This is an error in judgment: When you walk through that door, it's you the employer is going to see, not your resume. If you come in looking disheveled and out of place, your interviewer may find it hard to believe those claims you make on your resume about your attention to detail and consummate professionalism.

Spend an hour or two on your personal presentation, and you'll remind the employer of why you were called in for an interview, namely:

Career aspirations. No employer wants to waste valuable time on a candidate who doesn't seem interested in the job and prepared for the interview. Show that you care about the position by taking the time to look sharp, and make sure that your attire is consistent with the professional expectations of the position. This could mean that tousled, beachgoer hairdo may require a makeover—unless the job you've applied for is in outdoor education or the sports and entertainment industry, you don't want to convey to your employer that you're more serious about surfing than you are about stakeholder value.

Industry insight. Make sure your attire is industry-standard. If you come in to interview for a finance position looking like a comedian instead of a banker, you may not even last the 5 minutes it takes to make a case for your candidacy before being dismissed by an interviewer eager to move on to "serious" candidates who aren't sporting a fish necktie and rainbow suspenders. On the other hand, if you show up to interview for a comedy gig looking like a banker, your interviewers may feel like you're trying to make a joke they don't get—and you might lose the gig to a comedian whose humor is less esoteric.

Individual strengths. Look over your resume, and visualize the person described there. Is the innovative, award-winning graphic designer whose career you've outlined someone you'd expect to see in a boring gray flannel suit and white shirt? Is the licensed practical nurse with a decade of hands-on experience someone you'd envision in cowboy boots and impractically tight jeans? Consider your interview attire an outward reflection of your inner strengths, and let it be neither a costume that inadvertently disguises your professional capabilities nor a uniform that hides your individual strengths.

Attire

Aim for a look that's more spare and conservative than you would normally wear and a bit more formal than seems typical for employees in that organization, based on your background research. Candidates with insider information about the organization may be tempted to dress as its employees do, but that may be perceived as presumptuous by your interviewers. You haven't yet landed the job or earned the right to wear sneakers as long-time employees have. Plus, there's nothing like the sudden realization that you're seriously under-dressed to decimate your confidence. The accepted rule of thumb is to dress up one notch more formally than you would if you were to land this position.

Plan out your outfit at least 3 or 4 days before your interview, to leave yourself time to make any necessary wardrobe fixes. You might discover that your suit needs dry cleaning or that your stockings have a run. Model your entire interview outfit for someone else (preferably someone with impeccable judgment), and ask whether your look seems appropriate for the job, company, and industry for which you'll be interviewing. If your fashion consultant confirms any of your suspicions that something about your look seems to send the wrong message, make adjustments no later than the day before your interview—you don't want to be frantically shopping for socks the day of the interview. Then the night before the interview, lay out your clothes, jewelry, socks, and shoes and make sure it's all clean and free of rips, wrinkles, lint, loose buttons, and hanging threads. That way, you can rest assured you'll look your best.

Tips from Head to Toe

You will be looked over from head to toe in an interview, so groom yourself accordingly. Consider these tips for an appropriate interview look.

Hair. Tidy is the way to go, even if that entails styling products and a blow dryer. That doesn't mean you have to show up coiffed and lacquered like an anchorperson for the six o'clock news, but you shouldn't appear shaggy or (heaven forbid) show up with wet hair. Some additional considerations:

- **Short hair:** Short-haired women and men should appear clean and well-styled, with the back of the neck shaved as necessary for especially short looks. Hair that was trimmed no more than two weeks before the interview will give you that neat, kempt appearance you're aiming for in an interview.

- **Long hair:** Women with long hair may wear it down or pull it back in a barrette or a neat, but not overly elaborate, updo—you don't want your interviewer to be distracted with the thought "How did she do that with her hair?" Ribbons and glittery hairclips are to be avoided, since they're generally more appropriate to a high school cheerleading squad than a professional setting. Men with long hair do not have to chop their locks, as has been advised in the past—long hair for men is more widely accepted these days, though shoulder-length is generally considered the limit for most positions that don't include the words "rock star" in the job description. These conventions vary according to location, with long hair on men generally considered more acceptable in larger cities. Men with hair shoulder-length or longer should pull it back in a neat ponytail, and men with hair chin-length or longer should consider using styling products to keep it out of their face so as not to thwart the interviewer's attempts to look them straight in the eye.
- **Hair color and style:** While the thought of changing your hair for an interview may be anathema to you, understand that your interviewers could be so distracted by your army-style buzz-cut, George Clinton rainbow weave, or foot-high blue Mohawk that they might not hear everything you have to say. You might be used to looking at your radical hairstyle every day, but your interviewer may not have had that much practice—and like it or not, could have a hard time looking past your highly individual hair when picturing how you would fit in with the team or represent the organization and its culture to clients or constituents (especially in a risk-averse, conservative organizational setting such as a bank). This doesn't mean you have to "sell out" and look like someone you're not and never want to become. But if you don't want your hair to be the factor that makes or breaks your chances at a rewarding career, you might want to tone your signature hairstyle down a couple of notches—pull that vintage hairdo back in a barrette instead of a 1940s snood, or gather your dreadlocks in a tidy bundle at the nape of your neck.
- **The hair that's not on top of your head:** Men with facial hair should keep it well-groomed and short rather than bushy and are advised to adopt a contemporary but not overly trendy style. According to recent American workplace standards, goatees and narrow sideburns have graduated from unconventional to widely accepted; mustaches, long beards, and chin-strap beards tend to seem dated; and sideburns sculpted like lightning bolts are

likely to be viewed as trendy. Eyebrows should not be a distraction for interviewers, so you should groom them accordingly. You may startle your interviewer with hair in unexpected places too, so consider keeping that hair out of sight or groomed in accordance with current, culturally specific social conventions. For example, nose and ear hair should be trimmed for both men and women, since this may be considered unsightly by some interviewers. Women don't necessarily need to remove leg or armpit hair, but to avoid distracting their interviewer, women can always choose to wear pants or opaque stockings and shirts or dresses with sleeves.

Makeup. Unless you're pursuing a career onstage, there should be nothing particularly dramatic about your makeup. This means no brightly colored eye shadow, lipstick, or blush and no heavy mascara or eyeliner.

Jewelry. You don't want interviewers to be so blinded by your flashy accessories that they overlook your accomplishments, so keep jewelry understated. Remember the classic truism about accessories, and take off one piece of jewelry when you're fully dressed. In general, avoid jewelry that makes noise, such as bangle bracelets. If the shirt you are planning to wear requires cufflinks, be sure you have a pair to wear besides the novelty flamingo pair your Aunt Gladys gave you as a gag gift. Necklaces should be minimal and tasteful. For men and women alike, earrings should be smaller and simpler than you might wear typically, so as not to attract attention away from your eyes. Facial jewelry such as eyebrow hoops, lip studs, nose rings, or tongue studs should be kept to a minimum. Even in more progressive organizations, there is a generational gap in the United States when it comes to acceptance of facial piercings, so you might consider removing facial jewelry or wearing small, demure studs in place of heavy steel barbells or colorful jeweled hoops.

Case in Point: Being Yourself Is Not Always a Bad Thing

Making the tricky decision to remove a piercing, cut your hair, or purchase a suit may be an important decision for you to make in your job search—but before you take the leap, find out if it's actually necessary in the company, industry, and interview setting you're entering. Consider this case in point:

"I was just out of college and had splurged on two very conservative business suits—never mind the nose piercing, which I decided not to take out, since no employer I wanted to work for would demand that I remove it. I'd prepared an awkwardly large portfolio, too. But the interview that got me the job I wanted was conducted over the phone, so none of this mattered. I remember going for a jog, coming home, grabbing a beer, lighting a cigarette, and waiting for the phone to ring. There I was, sweaty, stinky, and basically doing things more appropriate to a bar than an interview, convincing these people to hire me. And hire me they did! I never wore the suits again; I eventually donated them to one of those charities that gives business attire to welfare recipients. The portfolio, now buried in my storage closet, is more a source of embarrassment than anything else these days. I'm not sure there's a good lesson in all this, but I learned that being relaxed in an interview is very effective, especially for people like myself who work in creative fields."

Nails. Your hands will be noticed by your interviewer at key times during the interview: when you shake hands, when you hand over your resume, and when you receive further reading material on the company. So be sure to make a good impression with hands that are clean and well-kept. Men's nails should be short and clean. Women should also have clean, shaped nails, and any nail polish worn should be neat and relatively inconspicuous. Women's nails should be short or mid-length rather than long—very long nails are usually impractical for office jobs.

Shirt. Men and women alike should inspect any shirt to be worn to an interview to make sure it's clean, wrinkle-free, stain-free, and shows no other obvious signs of wear such as holes, yellowed collar, frayed cuffs, or pulled threads. Women usually keep the top button of their shirt unbuttoned to convey a more relaxed, confident air, and men may opt to do the same in a more relaxed workplace setting. Women's shirts should not be overly revealing or show much skin below the clavicle bone, however, and men should wear undershirts under buttoned shirts to keep chest hair and pectoral muscles out of sight and off the interviewer's mind. The goal here is to make it easy for interviewers to keep their attention on your professional capabilities, rather than on your physical assets. Shirts should fit well and comfortably, without being clingy or constricting around the neck, bust, shoulders, or arms—you don't want to spend the entire interview fretting that you'll pop out of your shirt like the Incredible Hulk. Baggy shirts will show more wrinkles than ones that fit, so be sure you buy the right size. Whatever you do, don't make the mistake of wearing a shirt that isn't quite right and planning to wear a sweater or jacket over it for the duration of the interview. You just can't predict what the climate control in the interview room will be like, and this solution will only make you hot and uncomfortable when the pressure is on. You should always have a shirt appropriate to the season and climate (long sleeves for a Boston winter, short sleeves for Hawaii) and never settle for something that makes you feel itchy or awkward.

Neckwear. With the widespread acceptance of business casual attire in the United States, few professions require male employees to wear a tie every day anymore, and in some industries—such as technology, non-profit social services, arts, laboratory sciences, sanitation, entertainment, and advertising—it might even seem strange for men to wear ties in interviews unless they are applying for executive-level positions. But when in doubt of the industry and company standards on neckties, wise men resort to a tie for the interview. Men in more creative professions can afford to wear brighter and more boldly patterned ties, whereas men in more traditional fields might go for the classic regimental stripe or subtly patterned red "power tie." Women do not have such wardrobe constraints, but may choose to wear a simple necklace or scarf as an accent.

Jacket. Jackets are not always required in office settings and are seldom required in blue-collar jobs, but wearing them in an interview does give male and female candidates alike the advantage of a neat, structured, professional appearance. When selecting men's jacket fabric, take not only climate into account but corporate culture, too: tweeds and corduroy are more appropriate for academic, research, and scientific jobs than for cutting-edge technology companies or consulting firms. Denim and khaki are generally too casual as fabrics for interview jackets, either for men or women. Women have more latitude otherwise in terms of fabric or color, though white might leave you feeling overly concerned about where you sit or rest your pen. Be sure your jacket is clean and free of wrinkles, frayed cuffs, hanging hems, and loose buttons.

Outerwear. Since you will enter the office in your outerwear, your coat, scarf, gloves, hat, and umbrella may well be the first impression you convey. So make sure you show the same professionalism in your outwear as you do in the rest of your interview outfit. Double-check that there are no gaping holes, loose threads, stains, or unraveling seams; that it's all clean; and that the colors coordinate rather than clash.

Pants/Skirt. Contemporary and coordinating are what you're looking for in pants to wear to an interview. Your pants can be separates you've paired with a crisp shirt and coordinating jacket, or you can go the formal route and wear a suit. To keep your look contemporary, your pants should be flat-front instead of pleated, not too baggy, and not too tight. Khakis and jeans are too casual for most interview settings, so opt for a dark color or neutral shade of gray or brown—or for women, a neutral tone or color that matches your jacket will be flattering and appropriate. Women can choose to wear skirts, though they should not be more than an inch or two above the knee to keep the look appropriately professional, and they should be higher than ankle-length for mobility's sake.

Socks/Stockings. Men should wear dark socks to compliment their dress shoes, but women have more fashion choices (and dilemmas) in this regard. Novelty socks and brightly colored stockings are best avoided. Women used to be expected to wear flesh-colored pantyhose or sheer trouser socks, but now subdued neutral tones of black, brown, and charcoal in opaque or sheer stockings are widely acceptable. However, stockings should be only subtly patterned at most, and fishnet stockings are out of the question. Bare legs are often considered acceptable at workplaces in warm climates, as long as the skirt is long enough that you're not flashing as much leg as Marilyn Monroe over a sidewalk grate.

Shoes. Wear professional, polished, sensible, low-heeled shoes to your interview—sorry, those canvas athletic shoes and spike-heeled go-go boots just aren't appropriate unless you're an aspiring skateboarder or dancer. Whatever shoes you choose, be sure you've worn them at least a few times before the day of your interview—painful, blistered feet are one sure way to start your interview off on the wrong foot. Women have the option of wearing shoes in brighter shades than men can usually get away with in an interview setting, but are advised to be sure the color of the shoe isn't too loud and is the exact same shade as some other aspect of their outfit—such attention to detail won't go unnoticed and may boost your confidence too.

Case in Point: These Boots Were Made for Walking

Footwear may seem like a minor detail, but attention to detail is a key criterion for many employers. Consider the following case of an otherwise qualified applicant whose boots made her seem out of touch and out of place in the corporate world:

"We were hiring a research specialist to whip our corporate research and development center into shape, and it was my bright idea that rather than bringing in still more disorganized eggheads or consulting firm types with their incomprehensible acronym-based systems, we should try to hire an actual librarian to create a functional system. Unfortunately, only one librarian responded to our posting, and she arrived for the interview in a faded, flowered, ruffled shirt; clashing plaid kilt; and knee-high red rubber wading boots, carrying a battered manila folder with papers spilling out. It was the ultimate interview outfit fashion faux pas, like Paddington Bear meets the Nutty Professor! We finally hired a consulting firm guy whose acronym system actually made sense and whose shoes I can't remember—and perhaps that's as it should be."

Bring the Right Stuff

Leaving a good impression on your interviewers takes a certain amount of poise and grace, but it also takes the right equipment. Everyone knows to bring extra copies of their resume, but what really gives you a competitive edge is actual, physical evidence of what you've accomplished for other employers—and could do for your prospective employer. Consider the following possibilities.

Portfolio

Take a tip from the designers, advertising executives, and other creatives whose livelihood depends on their ability to sell their skills, and create a sharp professional portfolio of work that highlights your strengths and accomplishments. Whether you're applying for a job as a project manager or engineer, charts and graphs that show earnings or savings due to a project or process you implemented are sure to impress prospective employers. If your reports were published or you wrote a newsletter or sections of the annual report, add those to the portfolio too, along with any positive feedback you received. Stills of web pages you helped develop would be a terrific addition, particularly if you can supplement that visual with data on online sales, page views, site traffic, or other quantitative measures of your successful efforts. Create a "network map" of key relationships you helped your department or organization build by forging constructive relationships with key vendors, clients, other departments, new hires, investors, and you'll show the value you can offer your employer. In the back of the portfolio, include a narrative bio that sums up your strengths and work history in one paragraph, accompanied by a full curriculum vitae or resume.

Offer to walk your interviewer through your portfolio once he or she has had a chance to ask you a few general questions, and at the end of the interview offer to leave the portfolio behind to peruse over the coming week. By giving your interviewer a chance not only to hear about your accomplishments but to see them, you double your chances that your strengths will be remembered. Mention that you can stop by in a week or two to pick up the portfolio, since this gives you an additional point of contact with your interviewer to make a lasting impression. If you don't live near the office, provide a preaddressed, stamped envelope to return your portfolio—this shows your consideration for your interviewer's time and budget. But do be sure that there's nothing irreplaceable in the portfolio you leave behind.

Presentation

Since PowerPoint presentations have become an essential aspect of doing business for many organizations, why not show employers you come professionally prepared by creating a brief PowerPoint presentation for your interview? This is an especially good choice for those interviewing in a field that makes frequent use of PowerPoint presentations. For a first interview, you might opt to print out slides from a 5- to 10-minute presentation that you prepared for a previous employer or client.

Interviewers are likely to mention challenges facing the team, organization, or industry, so when you are invited in for a second or third interview, consider preparing a presentation focusing on sound, creative approaches to these issues. Print out handouts to accompany your presentation, and you'll give your employer another leave-behind that conveys your strengths.

If you do choose to prepare a presentation, be sure that it's a stellar example of the form. No one is likely to be impressed if you haven't mastered PowerPoint. If you've only learned the basics, leave this option to the PowerPoint jockeys out there.

Case in Point: Putting the Power in PowerPoint

Not every applicant will be thorough and thoughtful enough to listen closely to the organization's challenges and prepare a presentation, so you stand to gain the advantage by setting yourself apart. Consider this applicant's experience:

"When my current company invited me in for a second interview, they asked me to prepare a response to a case scenario likely to arise in the course of the job. So instead of walking in there and fumbling through index cards with my key points on them, I decided to present my response to the case on a 12-page PowerPoint and pass out handouts of each slide. It's not something the interviewers explicitly asked for, but I know at least one other candidate did something similar. It's not necessarily an interviewing requirement, but I think a presentation helps distinguish you as a serious candidate—after all, I got the job!"

Articles

Even the most skeptical, hard-to-please interviewer will be impressed by independent, third-party validation for your professional efforts in the press. So if you or your work have received favorable coverage in articles in trade publications, magazines, newspapers, or websites, by all means bring a photocopy of these clippings as a handout for your interviewers. If you're not sure whether your efforts have received media attention, run a Google search on your name, the names of organizations where you've worked, and the name of any products, events, accounts, or services you've worked on in the past. If you or your work has been favorably mentioned in multiple press stories, pick the ones that emphasize the professional strengths most pertinent to the position you hope to land, and provide a bibliography listing all the articles that show you and your work in a good light. With clippings and a bibliography to your credit, your candidacy will look even more impressive.

Make an Entrance

Your interview begins long before you meet your interviewer. Every person you meet from the moment you step through the door to the building may have the power to influence the decision to hire you: the doorman who chats every day with your prospective boss; the building security officers you ask for directions who are on a first-name basis with your future colleagues; the people on the elevator who may be your future team members; the receptionist who knows everyone in the organization; and that other woman in the bathroom who happens to be the administrative assistant to the head of the department. So beware of inadvertently snubbing any of these influential people by neglecting to say hello in a rush to get to the office, giving a curt response to an inquiry about the time, or forgetting to give thanks for directions to the right office. When asked what they thought of you, their response will at best be a lukewarm "OK, I guess"—and it could be much worse.

Being polite, friendly, and relaxed with everyone you meet is a great way to ensure a warm welcome into the organization. Approach people politely, look anyone you meet straight in the eye and offer a friendly greeting, apologize for interrupting if you need to ask a question, thank everyone who takes a moment to help you, don't hesitate to engage in conversation if someone approaches you or asks you a question, and mention that you've enjoyed your chat when you need to wrap up the conversation. Treat everyone with respect, and they'll reciprocate with a warm reception.

When you do meet your interviewer, you can follow a simple four-step protocol to get the interview off to a promising start. Here's a step-by-step breakdown:

1. **Get to your feet quickly** when your interviewer enters the room. Women aren't obliged to do this by custom as men are, but rising from your seat is a good way for both men and women to show eagerness to meet interviewers.

2. **Make eye contact** for at least a few seconds—don't just glance quickly, then glance away. You may do it because you're shy, but it's often interpreted as rudeness or aloofness. If you do look away, your interviewer may spend the rest of the interview wondering if there's something caught in her teeth. If your interviewer is a woman, keep your gaze strictly above the neck. Few mistakes can bring an interview to a grinding halt faster than a wayward glance that could be construed as a sexual advance. At the very least, you'll be remembered as the candidate who gave your interviewer the creeps, and this impression of you may be passed around in professional circles for some time to come.

3. **Smile—and mean it!** This person was intrigued enough by you to pick your resume out of a stack and is dedicating 30 minutes (often more) of a busy day just to talk with you—and with any luck, will soon be singing your praises to colleagues and possibly offering you a job. That's plenty to smile about.

4. **Shake hands firmly.** Not with fingers limp like wet noodles, but with a nice, firm grasp. Know your own strength, and don't cause your interviewer's eyes to water by squeezing too hard. A few seconds of shaking should do the trick—pump your interviewer's hand more than a couple times, and you may come across as desperate. If your palms are sweaty, subtly wipe your palm on your thighs as you stand to shake hands so that you don't offer a clammy handshake. Practice with a professionally savvy friend or two to find out whether your handshake seems about right to them.

Say It with Body Language

Nonverbal cues can be every bit as important to your interviewer as what you have to say. A brilliant remark can be undermined by a shy or uncertain delivery, and your interviewer may think you're making up your accomplishments if you avoid making eye contact while you're relating them. Throughout the interview, make sure that your body language conveys your confidence, openness, and enthusiasm.

Confident

Even if you occasionally look away, be sure you begin and end your responses by looking your interviewer steadily in the eyes for a few seconds. When you do look away, try to make sure your eyes aren't rolling upwards to the left or right, since this indicates you're grasping for ideas and distracts your interviewer with the thought, "Is there something hanging over my shoulder?" Try to keep your gaze at eye level, and by no means fixate on some physical part of your interviewer. There's a fine line between an absent-minded stare and a perceived offense, so be aware of where your gaze is aimed.

Your voice should also remain steady, and if you find it's beginning to shake, clear your throat and take a breath.

Open

Crossed arms indicate a certain wariness or defensiveness, and that's not how you want to approach your interviewer. Try keeping your hands in your lap, or hold a pen in one hand and your notepad on your lap with the other. Tightly crossed legs can make you appear inaccessible, and loosely crossed legs (with one calf resting on the opposite knee) may seem overly relaxed for an interview setting. Try to be conscious about not bouncing your knee either—this can make you appear eager to leave or go to the bathroom.

Enthusiastic and Alert

Some people get too nervous and fidgety. Some are mellow to the point of narcolepsy. But no matter the reason, there is never a good excuse for neglecting to show active interest in an interview. If you don't show genuine enthusiasm and engagement when meeting your interviewer and discussing the position available, your interviewer may justly conclude that you're just wasting both of your time.

Follow these simple tips for using body language to convey your enthusiasm.

Listen actively. Remember what your grandmother always told you and sit up straight in your chair. This makes you appear confident, alert, and interested in what your interviewer has to say. Try not to rest your head in one hand, as this can make you appear bored or sleepy.

Nod when appropriate, respond to your interviewer's comments with appropriate interjections or exclamations, crack a smile when your interviewer injects some humor into the proceedings, and ask questions for clarification when needed.

Give your undivided attention. Lean forward a little when your interviewer is speaking to show your interest. You don't need to stare intently at your interviewer the entire time, but you shouldn't be gazing idly at the ceiling or out the window while your interviewer is trying to make a point or pose a question. Always look directly at your interviewer when you begin to respond to a question, so that it's clear to whom you're addressing your remarks.

Case in Point: Attention, Please

If you're in a panel interview, make a conscious effort to share your attention with each of the interviewers so that no one feels slighted by inadvertent inattention. Consider the following case in point from a longtime career counselor:

"I can't tell you how often I've seen interviewees make the mistake of addressing their remarks exclusively to male interviewers on a panel, especially if they're white men. There's this subconscious belief that that's where the decision-making power lies, and that's certainly not always the case—I know I've always been hired by women, just as an example. Sharing your attention among multiple panelists can be a hard habit to learn, but it's essential in an ever more diverse workforce."

Be responsive. Don't let your expression become wooden or fixed, stare blankly, or zone out in the middle of your interviewer's commentary. Take notes periodically if that will help you stay engaged while your interviewer embarks on a particularly long monologue, but don't stare down at your notes the entire time or you might miss out on some nonverbal cue your interviewer is giving you: rolled eyes, a smile, a grimace.

Don't fidget. Your itchy scalp or stockings can wait—this interview is more important than any momentary discomfort. If you give in to a scratch more than once or twice in your interview, your interviewer is likely to think you (a) have got a nervous tic that indicates you might not be able to withstand the pressures of the job; (b) are impatient and can't wait for this interview to be over; or (c) recently contracted a skin disease that may be communicable and neglected to mention it before you shook hands.

Case in Point: Body Language Is a Two-Way Street

Interviewers may not always use body language you consider appropriate, and you'll have to use your best judgment about how to respond. If your instincts tell you an interviewer's intentions are not entirely above board, you may be better off wrapping up the interview as quickly as possible and moving on to more promising opportunities. Consider this nightmare scenario:

"I moved to New York City after graduation without a job lined up, but with big plans about finding a dream job in the film and video industry. I sent out dozens of resumes and discovered that no one was too interested in hiring a liberal arts grad with no work experience, so I began cold calling film and video production companies to see if they needed any freelance or permanent help. After a few dozen calls, I found a firm that was not looking for help now, but might be soon, and Mr. MightBeHiring asked if I could come in 'right now' for an interview. I threw on my interview dress, grabbed a cab, and arrived at the office—a loft in a mixed-use building. Mr. MightBeHiring himself answered the door wearing nothing but a towel around his flabby torso. A wise person would have turned and walked out right then, but I saw nothing but a job ahead, and the film industry was, after all, laid back, and he apologized profusely, saying he didn't think I'd get there THAT SOON. Mr. MightBeHiring went upstairs to 'change' and began conducting the interview over the wall while I sat downstairs. The interview went well, I thought, despite the unusual circumstance. We talked half an hour, and then he told me he thought it would work out. Yes, he said, you can come on up now. 'Let me show you the rest of the office.' Only when I reached the loft, Mr. MightBeHiring was completely naked and hiding in a back corner of the room. Needless to say, I got out of there quickly. I cringe whenever I think about that experience; things could easily have been a lot worse.

Build Rapport

Consider your interviewer's point of view: Would you rather hire the qualified candidate who easily engages you in conversation and would make a great team member and lunch partner, or the equally qualified candidate who is stony-faced and tense, and whose office you would probably approach with the same dread you would a dentist's? By the end of the interview, you want to leave visions dancing in your interviewer's head of what a delight it would be to work with you on a daily basis. No, this doesn't mean you should drug your interviewer—but you should do everything else in your power to put your interviewer at ease. This includes seeking common ground and showing your sense of humor.

Seek Common Ground

From your background research, you may already know of one or two things you have in common—an interest in scuba diving, say, or a background in marketing. Find a way to work these into the conversation, if your interviewer doesn't. Nothing establishes rapport like a shared passion or experience.

Be cautious when you proffer opinions, though, because you never know whether the book on gardening you found pointless might have changed your interviewer's life, or vice versa. Find some positive aspect of the book to comment on even if you weren't crazy about it, and be prepared to explain any reservations you express. If you're an avid fan of the book, avoid getting defensive if your interviewer offers a critique of it, and perhaps invite further details on the subject instead. Whenever points of commonality arise, explore them enthusiastically with follow-up questions.

Exhibit a Sense of Humor

Due to the judgment inherent in the process, interviews have the propensity to be anxiety-producing, awkwardly formal situations for everyone involved, so it is often a pleasant surprise and a huge relief when someone breaks the ice with wit or humor. However, off-color jokes are certainly not appropriate, and self-deprecating remarks, cheap gags, and painful puns may actually lower your estimation in an interviewer's eyes. Humor that is too highbrow can backfire, too. If you make a joke that's a complicated play on words or makes an erudite reference to Shakespeare, there's a chance the joke may go right over an interviewer's head—and no one likes to feel left out of a joke. Some interviewers may even misconstrue your meaning and think that you're making fun of them. So unless you're an aspiring comedian, stick to low-key jokes, and rely on humor only when it seems appropriate or necessary to break tension. And don't forget to laugh at the interviewer's jokes!

Master the Art of Q&A

After the obligatory introductions and preliminary chitchat with your interviewer comes the heart of the interview: the question and answer session. This is the part of the interview job seekers tend to dread most, but it doesn't have to be the grueling oral examination you may have imagined. In fact, the secret to mastering this part of the interview is to loosen up and make it a pleasant peer-to-peer *interaction* instead of a lowly-applicant-to-all-powerful-examiner *transaction*. In this exchange of ideas and insights, you should be interviewing your interviewer as a possible colleague, co-conspirator, and even friend, rather than appealing to a powerful entity to put you on the payroll. You share common interests in the organization and industry, and you are meeting to explore those shared interests and see how you might collaborate to address them. It's as simple as that.

Pay Attention to Clues

As long as you approach the interview as a dynamic interaction rather than a grilling session, you'll find there is no cause for panic. There are no magic right answers to any questions your interviewer may ask—only answers that are thoughtful, well-reasoned, and memorable. What's more, interviewers often provide clues about the kind of response they're looking for by asking leading questions. For example, let's say you're asked how you handle a particular project, and after your response the interviewer asks this follow-up question: "And how exactly might you involve the rest of the technology team in that process?" This is a strong hint that your interviewer considers involving the technology team important, and you should specifically address this concern in your response and in future responses.

Prepare for the Old Stand-Bys

Many interviewers don't have enough time to spare from their daily duties to dream up hard-hitting, unique interview questions, so they often resort to generic, tried-and-true stand-bys. You should always be ready to answer these common questions so you can provide exactly the kind of sharp, memorable responses your interviewers expect from a prime candidate.

Below are ten of the most common interview questions you'll come across in your job search. You'll notice that they're not necessarily good questions, but that should suit you fine—you can use a vague, ill-defined question to segue into a story that highlights one of your strengths.

1. Tell me about yourself.

What this really means: "I'm looking for personal insights about you that would make you seem less like a list of credentials and more like a person I'd like to work with every day."

Good answer: From my resume, you can see that I'm an experienced [job title] with [number] years in [field] and specialized expertise in [desired skill area]. But one thing you may not be able to tell from reading about me on paper is how [personal strength] I am when it comes to [requirement of job]. Just to give you an example, . . . [success story]."

2. What are the best and worst jobs you've ever had, and why?

What this really means: "Does this job match your ideal, or are you going to leave this job in 6 months for something better?"

Good answer: "When I was just starting out, one of my first jobs was as a [name position]. It was a tough job because of all the [job characteristic unrelated to job you're applying for] involved, but I stuck with it, and in the end I think it tested and strengthened my [personal strength] and gave me a greater understanding of how [job characteristic related to job you're applying for] works. So that job ultimately helped me become a better [job title], and land a great job at [company] that allowed me to hone my skills at [job requirement] and really focus on [area of job specialization]. On one project there, I was even able to . . . [success story]."

3. What project are you most proud of, and why?

What this really means: "What can you do for me and my organization?"

Good answer: Tell a success story related to the position, and wrap it up as follows: "That project resulted in [impressive numerical proof of success] for the company, but I'm particularly proud of the positive personal impact it made for our [key organizational constituency]. I heard from [number] of [key constituency] that our efforts changed the way they [positive feedback from others to demonstrate your success] for the better. One person even told me that [personal anecdote]."

4. What are your greatest strengths and weaknesses?

What this really means: "Prove to me that you'd bring value to this organization, and show me you're aware of and can learn from your mistakes."

Good answer: Again, mention a strength related to the position and illustrate it with an anecdote. Then follow this with a weakness that stems from inexperience rather than a lingering personality flaw. Show your knowledge of what's important to the industry, and describe what steps you're taking to work on it. Consider this example: "I learned the hard way that even if you're only required to submit invoices once a month, it's better to submit them the minute they come in to keep your key vendors happy. Vendors aren't going to tell you they're unhappy about getting paid more slowly, of course—they'll just take longer to respond to your requests. That's what happened to me in my last position with a graphic designer, right in the middle of a deadline push, and I ended up having to pull a team member off another task at the last minute to get the job done—not something I like to do to the team. In our business, reliable, responsive vendors are worth their weight in gold, so I'm learning to pay attention to these subtle signals to get the very best work out of vendors that I can."

5. Why did you leave your last position?/Why are you thinking of leaving your current position?

What this really means: "Was there any trouble with your last employer? Are you a chronic job-hopper?"

Good answer: If you were laid off, explain that "the position was eliminated as part of a broader shift in the business plan, as the organization shifted its emphasis from [business niche] to [another business niche]." That way, it's clear that you weren't dropped for not delivering enough value. That should be enough of an explanation to satisfy your interviewer—these days, everyone understands that downsizings usually aren't personal. If you were fired, briefly mention that "it wasn't a good fit" for reasons specific to the position. Don't blame it on personality conflicts, because you don't want to lead interviewers to speculate that you can't work well with others. Career changers who are making a shift "to pursue their true calling" should be prepared to show evidence of long-term interest in the field they're entering, so that employers don't think of them as career-hoppers. If you are considering leaving your current career "because this seems like too perfect a match for my skills in [specialization] and long-term interest in [field] to pass up," by all means say so—this is the kind of thing employers will be glad to hear.

6. Describe a time when you had to perform under pressure.

What this really means: "You're going to be asked to perform under pressure here, and I want to make sure you can handle it."

Good answer: Think of a high-pressure scenario your interviewer will relate to, and then describe how you handled it and the positive outcome you achieved. Just be sure that the situation you describe was not made difficult by factors in your control—you don't want interviewers to think you create needless drama in the workplace. For example, "Two weeks before a client's annual conference in Kansas City, there was a tornado that took the roof off of the hotel where attendees were supposed to be staying. But as any event planner knows, this is why you always have to have a plan B. I'd had a block of rooms in another hotel we regularly use for other events set aside in case of overflow, and by pulling a few strings I was able to expand the block to accommodate all the registered attendees. Another conference ended up having to cancel for lack of accommodations, but our conference went off without a hitch, and received high marks from attendees, too."

7. What kind of people do you enjoy working with most and least, and why?

What this really means: "How are you going to get along with me and/or the others on the team? Are you going to fit in with our corporate culture?"

Good answer: Think about what you know of the organization and the position before you answer. If it's a buttoned-down, conservative, financial setting, you might express your affinity with creative types as "people who are solidly grounded in their own business, but never lose sight of opportunities for competitive advantage" rather than for "wild-card, out-of-the-box thinkers." The reverse would be true for a more casual, creative environment. But because you never know if there will be exceptions to the rule on your future team, you should also mention that you get a lot out of working with people who have different styles and skill sets than you: "Because I'm [personality characteristic] myself, I find that I learn the most from people who are [personality characteristic]." If you're pressed to name a least-favored personality type, mention a universally unlikable type in an offhand way, "Well, I guess I wouldn't particularly enjoy working with a very mean-spirited person, but I've really never come across anyone in our line of work who fits that description—have you?"

8. Tell me about one success and one failure you've had in your career.

What this really means: "How do you measure success, and how do you handle setbacks?"

Good answer: Mention a success story that relates to the position, with numbers and anecdotal evidence of success to back you up. Then describe a failure that dates from early on in your career due to inexperience, and describe what you've learned from it. The mistake should be understandable, forgivable, unrelated to the job at hand, and have had no lasting consequences. For example: "One summer in college I had an internship as a lobbyist, and I was given a call sheet of 20 elected officials a day to call, along with talking points for each one. Unbeknownst to me, one day there was a glitch in the database, and all the talking points were mismatched. So there I was, passionately urging legislative aides about the importance of measures that weren't even in their district. The first two legislative aides on the other end of the phone sounded genuinely puzzled, and said, 'I'm sorry, the representative doesn't have a stance on this bill,' which I took as an invitation to press further. Finally on the third call, I spoke to an aide who said, 'I think you've got the wrong district.' I felt about an inch tall—but now I've learned my lesson not to think of technology as infallible, and to always check over my facts twice before I present them. It's helped me a lot in giving fundraising speeches for the last nonprofit I worked for, and saved me some heartache too!"

9. Where do you see yourself in 3 to 5 years?

What this really means: "Are you going to stick around so that we can reap the benefit of the training we'd invest in you?"

Good answer: Start off your response by saying: "Right here." Don't mention advancement right away, because you don't want your interviewer to think you'll be unhappy in the position and that you're really after someone else's job. Mention ways you hope you and the organization will grow in tandem: "I can see this department becoming a real profit center for the company with a growing consumer base among [target market], so I anticipate that I'll have an opportunity to further hone my skills within that market niche and possibly expand the department as we grow."

10. Why should I hire you over other qualified candidates?

What this really means: "Let's cut to the chase—what can you offer me that others can't?"

Good answer: This is your opening to reiterate your three strengths. Then close with a statement of your enthusiasm for the job: "I don't think you're likely to find another candidate who has my passion and commitment to this work, and that will be clear once we've had a chance to work together."

Anticipate Some Tough Questions

Even the best-crafted resume probably raises a few awkward questions about detours along your career path. Why did you leave that veterinarian's office after only 6 months? Why do you want to be a stockbroker now, after finishing vet school? What were you doing in that year off between your last position in finance and now? Don't get caught unprepared—have answers ready to questions about the following:

Gaps in employment. An unexplained gap of 6 months or more might raise questions in your interviewers mind about your commitment to your career or even your work ethic, so be prepared to address the issue head-on. Don't approach the issue defensively—"I was raising my kids, OK??"—but present your decision as a considered choice consistent with your long-term goals. Maybe you wanted to have kids sooner rather than later, so that you could concentrate on your career. A good explanation goes a long way—that decision to spend a year traveling around the wilds of Madagascar might be perfectly consistent with your interest in biodiversity and easily factored into your decision to pursue environmental law.

Layoffs and firings. In this economy, everyone knows someone who has been laid off or fired, and your interviewers might have been laid off or fired themselves at some point. So your interviewers are predisposed not only to understand termination of employment, but actually sympathize with this—provided you can discuss it without sounding bitter or accusatory. If you were laid off, you can simply explain that your position was eliminated as part of a broader institutional business decision—a restructuring, merger, or shift in the business plan—and leave it at that. No need to describe what a huge mistake it was or how sorry they ought to be. If you were fired, briefly explain why the role and/or organization just wasn't a good fit for you at the time, and leave personality and any pending lawsuits out of it. Mention any lessons learned or valued relationships you gleaned from your time in the position, and you'll sound the wiser for it.

Any stated qualifications not evident on resume. If you've mentioned that you're an accomplished writer put you have no bibliography of articles by you on your resume, explain why. Do you write speeches for your CEO that always get rave reviews from the audience? Have you written a grant as a volunteer that secured $20,000 for an after-school program? Bring up these accomplishments before your interviewer asks, to resolve any lingering doubts about your qualifications.

Evidence of job hopping. If you've had five positions in the last 3 years, your interviewer may have reason to suspect you'd leave the organization as soon as you get a better offer elsewhere. Explain the circumstances that precipitated so many moves and how those circumstances are different now. Maybe the frequent changes were the result of a combination of a downsizing, your spouse getting reassigned to another state, and taking some short-term contract positions while you were looking for the right job (this job, naturally!) to come along.

Inconsistent array of jobs. If it's not clear from your resume what you want to be when you grow up, you need to show your interviewer that there's a common thread in your interests. If you can explain that your career goal has always been to make a difference in kid's lives, suddenly it will make a lot more sense that you've been a track coach, a volunteer for the March of Dimes while you were pursuing a career in finance, and ultimately left your job as a banker to become a social worker for disabled children. Instead of being perceived as flaky, you'll come across as committed and well-rounded.

Career changes. Why should a florist hire someone who has spent most of his or her career to date as an auto mechanic? If this will be your first position in a new field, you need to explain how your skills and strengths are relevant to the position. You might explain that creative problem-solving and client interaction were always your favorite parts of your job at the body shop. And nothing wins over an interviewer like a shared passion—the money was great as an auto mechanic, but you knew from the first time you walked into an ikebana class that you'd found your true calling, even though it meant that you'd have to start over in a new field from the bottom up. With an anecdote like that, who wouldn't want to give you a shot?

Money, money, money. Perhaps the trickiest question you might be expected to answer in an interview is when you're asked how much you'd expect to be paid for the position. Most interviewing experts agree that you want to avoid being the first person to name a number, if at all possible. There are a number of potential responses to the initial salary question. Here are just a few:

- I'm willing to entertain any fair offer.
- I've learned a lot about the position today, and I'd need to take some time to think about the roles and responsibilities described before I can arrive at an answer.
- There are a number of elements that make up a compensation package, so I prefer not to discuss salary in isolation. Can you describe a typical compensation package?

It's best to wait as long as possible to discuss salary—preferably after you've convinced your potential employer that you're the only choice. The best leverage you have in the salary discussion is their desire to hire you.

When it is time to discuss salary, be sure that you have researched median salaries for the relevant position, industry, and geographic location. Your research should enable you to complete this sentence: "I know [$X to $X amount] is the standard salary range for a [position] in [geographic location], and given my [years of experience, specialized training/degree, skill set], I'd expect to come in at the [middle/upper] end of that range." Never suggest that you belong on the rock-bottom end of the pay scale, even if you're just starting out; you need to communicate your value to the organization.

For a more in-depth discussion of salary negotiations, turn to *The WetFeet Insider Guide to Negotiating Your Salary and Perks.*

Remember That It's a Conversation

The most important (and difficult) thing to remember in crafting appropriate responses to interview questions is that this is really just a conversation, so keep it conversational. Lengthy monologues and curt yes or no answers would be considered rude in any conversation, so avoid them in an interview, too. Role-play your responses to a few questions you expect your interviewer to ask with a friend and a stopwatch, timing yourself to make sure your answer is not too short (under 30 seconds) or too long-winded (longer than 2 to 3 minutes). But though you may want to jot down a few points you'd like to make and questions you'd like to ask, don't memorize your answers or spend all your time staring at your notepad. You run the risk of sounding too rehearsed or phony, and you want to be responsive to your interviewer and allow your personality to shine through in your off-the-cuff remarks.

Case in Point: Watch for a Spark

Gauge your interviewer's interest in what you have to say, and tailor your responses accordingly. Take this tip from a senior manager who's spent quality time on both sides of the interview table:

"I always talk to interviewers with the same interest that I would getting to know someone at a party that I'm interested in knowing. This means paying attention to details, the words they use, inflections, the questions they ask—it's really just like any other social interaction. I follow their lead in the conversation, and watch them as they speak and listen to my response. If I see them spark with an idea I've brought up, I explore it; if not, I drop it. I'm not going to spend 10 minutes going on about something they have no interest in, even if it's the hottest, newest thing in business. It's all about building rapport, and not at all about giving the 'right' answer—that's too stilted and two-dimensional."

Focus Your Response

Some questions may seem tough to answer at first. Since interviewers get nervous and flustered, too, they may ask questions in a roundabout or long-winded way. If you're not quite sure what is being asked of you, by all means ask your interviewer for clarification. Ask for confirmation of what you think you heard, with a query that begins: "Let me make sure I have this right. . . ." Your interviewer also may present you with complicated case questions and detailed hypothetical scenarios, and in this situation you may want to buy yourself a little time by briefly (30 seconds or less) summarizing the case and seeking confirmation on those details before giving your answer. Try to keep your responses focused and succinct, so that your interviewer does not lose interest or begin to think of you as someone who is big on talk but short on concrete solutions. If you get the sense that your interviewer is dissatisfied with your answer or is looking for more, you can invite further input with a follow-up query such as, "Does that answer your question?"

Deflect Inappropriate Questions

The most awkward questions, of course, are those that are utterly inappropriate in an interview. If your interviewer asks a personal question that seems intrusive to you, politely give your interviewer a way out by saying, "I'm sorry—I'm not sure I understand the question." If your interviewer repeats the question instead of dropping it, you can choose to respond or attempt to return the conversation to less personal topics by saying, "Why do you ask? Do you expect that this will come up in the course of the job?" That puts the onus on the interviewer to explain the point of the question. If the interviewer persists and you still feel extremely uncomfortable answering the question, you can always graciously evade the question by saying with a smile, "Well, to be honest, I feel put a little on the spot talking about this since we've only just met. . . . You know how that is." And know that no matter what, you are not obliged to answer any illegal questions along the lines of those listed in the table. (For more resources on this subject, see the For Your Reference chapter at the end of this book.)

Questions You Shouldn't Have to Answer

According to Human Resources Powerhouse, any of the following questions about an applicant's "protected characteristics" could provide grounds for a legal discrimination claim:

Are you a U.S. citizen?

What is your nationality?

Have you ever been arrested?

Have you ever filed for bankruptcy?

Do you have a physical or medical condition?

Are you married?

What are your child care arrangements?

Are you a member of a union or labor organization?

Have you ever sued a former employer?

Have you ever filed a workers' compensation claim?

What were some of the problems in your last job?

When did you graduate from college (or high school)?

Are you available to work on Easter Sunday?

Are you planning on starting a family?

What type of military discharge did you receive?

Source: HR Powerhouse. www.hrpowerhouse.com.

Getting Down to Brass Tacks: Interview Types

- Phone Screen
- Online Screen
- Job Fair Interview
- Office-Visit Interview

Now you're equipped for your interview—but what kind of interview will that be? Different interview types require slightly different strategies, so review the types described in this chapter and plan your approach accordingly.

Phone Screen

Many job seekers think of a phone screen as a formality: The employer is clearly interested, so all you have to do is sound relatively competent and set up an in-person interview, right? Wrong. This is actually a first-round interview, and you should be prepared to make a stellar impression over the phone just as you would if you were meeting in person. But instead of having a week to prepare yourself, you may be expected either to respond to questions on the spot or to set up a conversation in a day or two at most. So, you'll need to review the job posting carefully and do as much interview prep as you can in the time allotted. Then you're ready to follow these ten steps to phone-screen success.

1. Have a professional-sounding outgoing voice-mail message.

Imagine you're an employer looking to fill a midlevel manager position, and you're taking a chance by calling a candidate who doesn't have much management experience, but seems capable enough to take on added responsibility. How do you think you'd react to an outgoing message of your promising candidate singing, "I'm wasting away again in Margaritaville—can't get to the phone"? You probably wouldn't even bother leaving a message. The moral of this story?

Record a professional-sounding message in your voice with no singing, no gimmicks (e.g., a message recorded by your 4-year-old cousin), and no slang ("Yo, what up?" is out, and so is "Howdy—leave a message, y'all!").

2. Express appreciation for the call.

Even if you're caught completely off guard by the call, be welcoming and enthusiastic. "Hello. I'm so glad you called!" Smile when you say it—the person at the other end of the phone can't see your expression but will be able to hear the warmth in your voice.

3. Make sure it's the right time and place.

Maybe you get the call while you're at work, with your boss breathing down your neck for that quarterly earnings report and your colleagues hounding you for the latest sales figures. Or the phone rings when you're telecommuting from home, with kids in the kitchen yelling to make themselves heard over the sound of the automatic ice-maker. Either way, this is not the ideal scenario for a phone interview—you need to be able to give your interviewer the benefit of your full attention, without any distractions.

So when the interviewer catches you at a bad time and asks, "Is this a good time to talk?" your response should be something along these lines: "Actually, is there a time I can reach you tomorrow or the day after? I'm very interested in the position and I want to give you my undivided attention, but I'm afraid now isn't the best time." Make plans so you can receive the call in a quiet place where you won't be interrupted. Ask the interviewer to reach you at home where you'll be more free to talk, and send your roommates out for pizza if you have to.

4. Be sure you're speaking on a land line.

A poor cell phone connection can leave both parties feeling frustrated, and you don't want to inadvertently hang up on your interviewer. If you're speaking on your cell phone, ask if you can call your interviewer right back on your land line.

5. Have your resume, notes, and datebook in front of you.

Your interviewer may ask you specific questions about your work history, and giving vague answers will not make a good impression. The phone screen is like an open-book exam: You can have all the notes you need right in front of you. Your cheat sheet should include:

- Explanations for any inconsistencies in your work history.
- An anecdote about each of the past positions that are most relevant to the one you've applied for.
- Stories outlined and ready to relate about your strengths, weaknesses, and proudest accomplishments.
- A few questions about the position and the company to demonstrate your interest and enthusiasm.

Don't inquire about money or benefits just yet, unless your interviewer asks you about your salary point-blank—now is not the time for you to negotiate. Finally, be sure to have your calendar handy so you can set up an in-person interview right away.

6. Be an active listener.

Hear out your interviewer's questions in full, without interrupting, and make sure you ask follow-up questions for clarification if need be. Your interviewer cannot see you nod, and may interpret your silence at the end of the phone as a dropped line—so be sure to interject the occasional active listening cues, such as "I see," "right," "OK," "that's interesting," and "absolutely." Give your interviewer the benefit of your undivided attention. This means switching off the television or radio and not making distracting noises by chewing gum or rustling papers.

7. Expect elimination questions to come first.

Unlike in-person interviews, phone interviews often cut right to the chase, without a lot of preliminary chitchat. Prepare for tough, awkward questions to be asked right away, such as:

- Why do you want to work for us?
- Why did you leave your previous job(s)?
- What are your greatest strengths and weaknesses?
- What's one problem you wish you had handled differently at your last job?
- What traits do you like most and least in a supervisor?
- What salary would you expect in this position?

8. Avoid verbal tics.

You know how some people, when they're, like, all nervous and stuff, say things in a way that, ummm, makes them sound, you know, kind of, well, less than professional? Be aware of your verbal mannerisms on the phone, since your interviewer will have few other cues by which to judge your professionalism. If you know you tend to hem and haw, practice with a friend over the phone until you can make your case clearly and succinctly, without mumbling, speaking too quickly, or clearing your throat often. Tape yourself, and note how many times you say "umm," "like," and "you know," and make an effort to decrease such verbal tics in future practice sessions.

Another verbal tic that interviewers tend to associate with younger, less experienced candidates is "upswing," a tendency to have the cadence of the voice rise as though every sentence (or portion of a sentence) ends in a question mark. For example, listen to yourself say this out loud: "Then I worked in London for 3 years? and as you'll notice on my resume? I was promoted twice? so by the time I left, I was in charge of a team of ten?" With upswing, this statement sounds much more dubious and less impressive than if you said it using a more factual, even cadence: "Then I worked in London for 3 years, and as you'll notice on my resume, I was promoted twice—so by the time I left, I was in charge of a team of ten."

9. Earn your 15 minutes in the spotlight.

With in-person interviews, most interviewers will grant you at least 15 minutes out of sheer politeness, even if you're clearly not the right fit for the position available. But over the phone, interviewers feel much freer to abruptly terminate interviews that don't seem promising. So don't save your best stories for last—make a favorable impression early on, and do your best to maintain it throughout the phone call.

When you answer your interviewer's questions, make sure that you are direct and to the point, try not to ramble or flounder, don't exaggerate or downplay your experience, and tell stories that present your abilities in a positive light. Instead of answering yes or no questions with a single word, follow up with a comment about your past experience. For example, instead of responding "Yes," to the question, "Are you comfortable occasionally working weekends?" you might say, "Yes—in fact, during my time as a public relations rep, I worked most weekends."

10. Inquire about next steps.

When the interviewer takes steps to conclude the interview by thanking you for your time or asking whether you have any additional questions, respond with, "I'm very interested in the position, and I would like to know about the next steps in the hiring process. Could we set up a time to meet in person?" Even if your interviewer does not seem particularly enthusiastic during the interview, you should still ask—HR reps in particular are trained to give as little indication of interest as possible, to test your perseverance and to avoid raising any candidate's hopes prematurely. If your interviewer declines your offer to set up an interview on the spot, ask when you should follow up.

Finally, enthusiastically thank your interviewer again for taking the time to call. Your graciousness, appreciation, and interest will leave a positive impression.

Case in Point: Be the Answer to Their Prayers

If you think a phone screen is stressful, consider your interviewer's point of view: Most managers who do phone screens probably have dozens of other items on their to-do lists for the week and would like nothing better than to wrap up this candidate search and get on with their previously scheduled work program. Be the calm in the storm of your interviewer's hectic schedule, and you may win yourself the job. Consider this advice from a gainfully employed individual who has survived many a phone screen:

"If a manager is taking time out of a busy day to call me, I know it's because they really, really need help. They've probably put off hiring far too long already, and now they probably only have time to meet with the three or so top candidates. So I'm always calm and reassuring, and I ask them how they'd describe the most pressing demands of the position. Once I've heard this, I respond by saying, 'That sounds manageable to me. I've been in the business for 10 years now, so this would not be the first time I've handled that kind of situation. . . .' Then I go on to describe a time I've faced a similar problem to the one the interviewer described, and achieved a good outcome. I keep the conversation positive and low-key. You can sometimes hear the sigh of relief at the end of the phone! This is a good sign—if the manager sees you as the solution to their problems, you'll land the job."

Online Screen

Rather than weed through stacks of resumes to fill technical or administrative positions, many employers are narrowing down their lists of viable candidates with automated online forms or tests. These tests use answers entered, keyword searches, and red-flag questions to sort candidates according to skills, experience, and expectations. Sometimes these tests aren't even reviewed by an HR representative until after they are put through an automated sorting process to screen out tests with undesirable responses to yes-or-no questions. Since these forms are Web-based, an unexpected technical glitch or lapse in the Internet connection could mean your answers are wiped out. To make sure you don't have to recomplete the entire form from scratch, you might want to fill your answers out in a word-processing document (or on good old-fashioned paper) before cutting and pasting or copying them into an online form. Using this method will also allow you to run spell-check on your answers before you paste them into the form.

Take extra care when crafting your responses, since you can't backtrack in writing the way you can in conversation. Always read the questions carefully to be sure you understand each one, the directions provided, and ratings scales—online screens are intended to test your attention to detail. When you craft your response, think strategically about what you are saying. Mistakes made are irrevocable once you hit the send button, so read over each answer once for content and once for spelling before you submit them. Below is an example of a Web screen for a senior administrative position, along with hints about what answers might qualify or disqualify candidates for the job.

Sample Web Screen

1. Why are you interested in leaving your current position, or why did you leave your most recent position?

Red light: "Bored" or "Got fired" are probably not the best answers, since these may raise red flags for the screener, and get your application tossed onto the "no" pile after the first question.

Green light: Instead, try a longer explanation without red-flag buzzwords: "Having effectively managed a three-person team for 2 years, I'm ready to take on responsibilities for a larger team and further hone my strengths in personnel management." Another option: "My position became redundant after a merger that changed the business model of the company and eliminated all support staff positions."

2. What is your current or most recent salary?

Red light: Inflating your salary. Your employer can easily find out if you're telling the truth by checking your references.

Green light: Tell the truth—but don't be afraid to ask for a higher salary than your current one, either (see next question).

3. What salary are you seeking?

Red light: Asking for the same amount or less than you're currently paid for a position of equal responsibility—you'd be discounting your value before the employer has gotten to know your merits. Unless this position comes with much less responsibility than your previous position, always ask for more than what you were paid at your last position, in accordance with industry standards for your years of experience, geographic location, and other factors. This shows that you are aware of the value you add to the organization.

Green light: Provide a salary range that starts from just above your current pay scale to one notch higher, and explain the reason for your answer in terms of standard salary ranges. For example: "Since this position comes with greater responsibilities than my current position, I would expect the pay to be higher. The salary range I propose is in accord with industry standards for this position." Here's another example: "Since my last position was at a non-profit organization, the salary standards were below industry average for equivalent positions in the for-profit sector. In a private-sector company, I would expect my salary to reflect industry averages for the position in for-profit enterprises."

4. Has your current position or a recent job required you to support more than one individual on a daily basis?

Red light: If they're asking, it must be important—a "no" answer could disqualify you.

Green light: Think about how many people you support regularly: your immediate supervisor(s), senior executives, cross-functional team leaders, and co-workers. Count them carefully—your interviewer may double-check this number with your references.

5. Please rate the frequency with which you use the following skills in your current position (or used them in your most recent relevant position if currently in a career transition), using the following scale:

1 = daily or almost daily

2 = weekly or almost weekly

3 = monthly or almost monthly

4 = quarterly or almost quarterly

5 = rarely if ever

___ Drafting, editing, and proofreading professional correspondence

___ Creating/developing presentations

___ Creating/preparing reports

___ Coordinating meeting arrangements

___ Creating and maintaining databases and spreadsheet files

___ Coordinating and assisting implementation of website updates

___ Coordinating, proofreading, and distributing e-mail newsletters

Red light: Don't jot down all 1s and 2s to impress a potential employer with your multi-tasking abilities, unless it's actually true. Remember that after you're hired, you will be expected to live up to the reputation you've built for yourself!

Green light: Stay true to your experience. Even if you don't update websites often in your current job, you may be able to develop those skills in your new job.

6. Please rate your level of expertise with each of the following technologies on a scale of 1 to 5, as follows:

1 = expert

2 = professional competency

3 = basic proficiency

4 = some familiarity

5 = unfamiliar

(Note: In addition to a number, please give an example of a task or project that has required you to use and further develop this skill.)

____Word

____FileMaker Pro

____Excel

____PowerPoint

____Crystal Reports

____HTML

____XML

Red light: If you're looking over this list of technologies and thinking, "I don't know half of those technologies," don't despair. As long as you have a firm grasp of the technologies typical for the position (e.g., Word and databases for administrative positions), you should still be a viable candidate. The list provided here includes many technologies that are not typically expected of administrative specialists—for example, XML is a complex computer language more commonly required in tech positions—this list probably represents the company's wish list of technological skills.

Green light: Go with what you know. Some familiarity is obviously better than none if they're asking, but it's better to be honest up front so you don't have to give yourself a crash course in Crystal Reports before you're brought in for an interview and tested on it.

7. In case we wish to conduct a telephone interview with you, what number should we use to reach you during normal business hours (8:00 a.m. to 5:00 p.m. Central Standard Time), and what is the best time of day to contact you?

Red light: Providing a work phone number that goes through the receptionist instead of directly to your desk. Imagine how that page might sound: "Betsy, our company's biggest competitor is holding for you on line two." Your colleagues will surely wonder what you're up to—not to mention your boss.

Green light: If you're currently employed, you might provide a cell phone number and request that the prospective employer call you during your lunch hour, so that you can speak more freely.

8. If we decide to bring you in for an in-person interview, how much lead time do you need to make arrangements to come in for an interview?

Red light: Saying "2 days" to be accommodating, when that means you might have to take an expensive, uncomfortable red-eye flight to get to an interview for a job you might not get. On the other hand, a month is probably too much to ask for—the employer needs to fill the position, and can't afford to wait around for you forever.

Green light: Be reasonable. If you're local and you have a flexible schedule, there's no reason not to say 2 days. But, if you're not local, 2 weeks should be enough to get a reasonably priced ticket and make arrangements for someone to cover you for a day at work, if need be.

9. If you live outside of commuting distance from our company headquarters in Boulder, Colorado, please answer the following questions:

Why are you thinking about relocating to Boulder?

Would you expect the company to pay your relocation expenses?

Red light: "I love to ski" is clearly the wrong answer to the first question, even if it's an important reason for you. "For this job" may seem appropriately enthusiastic, but it's an insufficient answer. The company is probably asking this question because they are concerned about turnover; they don't want to hire people who love their job but can't stand the weather, or otherwise discover that they are ill-suited to life in Boulder, and vacate their positions quickly.

Obviously the company would rather not pay relocation expenses, if they are taking the time to mention it here. The second question is also something of a catch-22: If you have some other reason for moving to Boulder other than the position, why should the company pay for your moving expenses?

Green light: For the first question, try an answer that demonstrates your familiarity with or connections to the area. For example: "This position is a big draw for me. I also have family in Colorado, and it has become a priority for me to live nearer to them." You can also use your research on the area to appeal to your prospective employers' civic pride: "This position would be a major impetus to relocate, but Boulder has long appealed to me and my family on its own merits as one of the most highly rated small American cities for its quality of life, many cultural activities, and of course the scenic setting. We have been contemplating a move from Detroit to a smaller city for some time now, and this position offers a prime opportunity to take the logical next step to Boulder."

Both of these answers name the position as the prime reason for moving, so it's legitimate for you to suggest that the company cover some of your costs if it is within their budget to do so. Here's how you might word that suggestion: "A modest moving stipend would be helpful to defray some of the relocation costs to be incurred, if such a stipend is available."

Other Online Screening Forms

The preceding example is the type of brief, basic screen you are most likely to come across as a candidate for nontechnical, nongovernmental positions in the United States, but online screens for technical and governmental positions and jobs overseas can be much more laborious. Online screens for technical positions often include a section that tests proficiency with specific technologies (e.g., Oracle databases, programming languages such as Java) or understanding of technological functions (e.g., networking). Technology companies may also use online screens to test your interest in and knowledge of their company, in addition to their products and applications. Forms for governmental positions may include questions intended to assess your eligibility for security clearance and may also test the specific skill sets required for the positions. (Some U.S. governmental agencies, such as the Foreign Service, require all candidates to take a rigorous exam before their applications will be considered.) Positions overseas may be subject to different labor laws and require knowledge of languages other than English, and these requirements may be reflected in online screening forms.

Job Fair Interview

Don't let the name fool you: Job fairs are not all fun and games. The HR representatives and recruiters with booths at the fair may be all smiles, but they have serious business to attend to: identifying a limited pool of qualified applicants from the ocean of job seekers.

Job fairs aren't just for young 'uns, either; anyone considering switching careers or industries or simply expanding their career horizons might benefit. (However, if you're currently employed, you may not want to advertise the fact that you're attending a job fair.) Look for job fairs in your region organized by local universities or non-profit professional associations around a specific theme (e.g., jobs overseas or public service opportunities) or industry of interest to you. These are often open to the public for a modest entrance fee (usually less than $150, and even less for students). You should be able to check the list of organizations scheduled to attend and identify some you might like to target in your job search.

Why Bother?

There's a common misunderstanding that the best companies don't need to recruit at career fairs, and that job fairs are completely divorced from the hiring process. On the contrary, some companies refer candidates to career fairs as a first step to getting taken seriously as a candidate, especially for entry-level positions. Few organizations actually hire on the spot at career fairs, it's true—but a successful job fair screening can catapult your candidacy to the top of the heap of applications that flood appealing organizations. It's not just computer companies that recruit at career fairs, as is commonly believed; a career fair might be a great place to get your start in any of the fields listed in "Industries that Recruit at Career Fairs."

Industries that Recruit at Career Fairs

Industry	Company Types
Biotech	Agricultural and pharmaceutical companies, biotech research and development laboratories, biomedical research institutions
Consumer goods	Food and beverage manufacturers, major retail chains, fashion merchandisers
Engineering	Environmental engineering firms, consulting and construction firms, aerospace companies, governmental research and monitoring agencies, non-profit advocacy organizations, utility companies
Entertainment	Talent and literary agencies, publishing houses, entertainment conglomerates, special effects studios, video game companies
Finance	Investment banks, stockbrokerages, financial services companies, venture capital firms
Government	Education, parks, Peace Corps
Non-profit agencies	Direct service providers, research institutes, advocacy organizations, cultural/arts organizations, religious charitable organizations
Technology	Computer/software companies, technology systems/infrastructure service providers, online retailers, wireless and satellite technology companies, semiconductor manufacturers

More Than a Face in the Crowd

One glance at the crowds at a career fair, and you might think that making an impression on a prospective employer is a long shot in this setting, . . . at least when you send in your resume for a position, you don't have to come face to face with your competition! But if you can give an employer a good reason to remember you at a job fair, your resume is a lot less likely to languish at the bottom of that big stack. Here are eight tips to make that happen:

1. Target three organizations. Go over the list of organizations that will be in attendance, and identify at least three booths you want to be sure to visit. (If there aren't at least three, you may want to reconsider ponying up the entrance fee for this particular job fair.) Then do some background research on each of these organizations as described in Getting Ready, identifying competitive pressures, key opportunities, and major milestones for that company. Jot these down on a notepad to take with you, and then add three questions to ask each target organization. Know your answers to the ten most commonly asked interview questions, and do some research to identify FAQs for organizations in your chosen field (see previous chapter).

2. Bring four (yes, four!) versions of your resume. Tailor your resume for each of your three target companies, and print out a couple copies of each tailored resume to hand out at the appropriate booth. Then print out several copies of your standard, all-purpose resume for positions in your field. Make sure you direct the correct version into the proper hands.

3. Map out your plan of action. Locate the booths for your target organizations on the map of the job fair so that you can find them easily amid the throng. But instead of planning to make a beeline for your target booths, make arrangements to arrive early so that you can warm up with a round or two of interviews at other booths before you approach any of your targets.

4. Browse through handouts. If there's a crowd around the booth when you approach or a line to speak with recruiters, bide your time patiently and productively looking through the literature on hand. You may think of other pertinent questions or come up with an insightful comment to open a conversation from something you read in the brochure, media clipping, or annual report.

5. Strike up rewarding conversations. Recruiters are required by their employers to screen many candidates at a job fair, but you make their job easier and set yourself apart by approaching them proactively with a relaxed, confident, friendly manner. Check over your notes before you approach your target booths, so that you're not left awkwardly fumbling through papers when you should be making an up-close and personal career connection. Remember that this is an interview, no matter how relaxed or rushed it may seem, so you'll want to carry yourself with the same professional demeanor from the minute you approach the booth that you would walking into the office of a prospective employer. And as always, greet your interviewer with a handshake, smile, and at least a few seconds of steady eye contact.

6. Work up an elevator pitch. Prepare a 30-second monologue that sums up your interests and strengths in the field, and your interest in the organization in particular, then turn the conversation over to your interviewer with an informed question. As an example, try filling in the blanks in this spiel:

"I studied/worked as a [position title] at [name of university/organization], which was great because it allowed me to hone my skills in [name of discipline]. I found that I particularly enjoyed [specialty area], so I'm excited to learn more about how I might make use of my abilities in [name of discipline] while pursuing my interests in [specialty area]. That's why I wanted to seek you out today. I know [name of organization] is well-respected in the [name of discipline] field, and I'm curious: In the future, what role do you think [specialty area] might play in your organization and the industry overall?"

7. Make good use of your time—and the interviewer's. Plan to go early and stay through lunch late into the day, so that you don't miss the opportunity to chat at length with representatives of your target organizations when the crowd thins out. Some organizations may have to pack up early, though, so don't put off visiting your target organizations too long. Don't take up too much of the interviewer's time or ramble on, especially if the lines are long behind you. Stick around for 10 minutes or until your interviewer begins to lose focus on you, and then offer to pick up the conversation later. A graceful exit goes something along these lines: "I don't want to keep you, but this is a fascinating discussion. Maybe we can chat more later today, when things are a bit less hectic for you?" If the interviewer agrees, stop by later and at least say hello, offer thanks for the conversation, inquire about next steps in that organization's hiring process if you're interested. Some interviewers may even set up a longer interview later in the day for you.

8. Gather key information. Be sure you get a business card so that you can follow up on your conversation later. Make notes immediately after each conversation so that when you send a thank-you note later, you'll be able to refer to a specific insight or comment your interviewer shared with you.

Office-Visit Interview

Last but far from least is the type of interview that looms largest in our imaginations: the office visit. And with good reason, too—office-visit interviews are one step closer to getting hired than job fair screens or phone screens. If you've diligently done your homework and taken the preparations outlined in the preceding chapters, you should be set to impress in your office-visit interview.

That said, you may have to go through several rounds of office-visit interviews before an actual job offer is made. The approaches to these office-visit interviews may vary too: The first meeting might be a one-on-one behavior-based interview with an HR rep, the second a job simulation, and the third a panel interview. Or you might find that you have to go through several rounds of interviews using different approaches in one day. So take a deep breath, pace yourself, make sure you have a firm grasp of the various types of office-visit interview approaches outlined in the sections that follow, and prepare to go the distance between that first step across the threshold and the final handshake that confirms your employment.

Behavior-Based

One of the most widely accepted axioms about human behavior is that the best indication of future behavior is past behavior, so it should be no surprise that the behavior-based approach is the most common type of office-visit interview. This approach probes your potential to make positive contributions to the organization in the future by asking you to define past contributions you've made to teams, organizations, and volunteer efforts.

What to expect. Most behavior-based questions will begin with: "Can you tell me about a time when you . . ." "Please describe an instance where you . . ." "Could you give me an example of a situation when you . . ." When you hear this cue, know that you are being asked to relate a specific anecdote that shows how you applied your talents to help an organization tackle a problem or make the most of an opportunity. Your answer will be judged according to set criteria that you can remember as the "Straight A's" of behavioral interviewing:

- Analyzing the opportunity or problem effectively
- Approaching the opportunity or problem creatively, to overcome major obstacles
- Accessing appropriate team resources to implement solutions
- Achieving concrete results, with figures wherever possible

Sample behavioral questions.

1. Please tell me about a time when you had a conflict with someone and how you handled it.
2. Can you describe an instance when you had to juggle several tasks at once, and describe how you prioritized your work?
3. Can you give me an example of a time when you took the initiative to seize an opportunity your organization might have missed otherwise?

Special preparations. Now all your hard work preparing brief anecdotes to highlight your strengths will pay off. Be sure to focus on achievements that will be relevant and meaningful to the organization, and describe them in terms your interviewer will understand. For example, if you used to produce a television show and you're making the jump to commercial advertising, you may want to focus on how your programming changes helped hit the show's target market, as demonstrated by increased viewership for the show and advertising dollars, rather than how many complimentary e-mails you received. But don't make your story straight facts, figures, and industry jargon, or your interviewer's eyes are sure to glaze over. Make your story a rollicking adventure of trials, tribulations, and triumphs. Consider this example:

"When I started working at Channel Z News, it was the lowest-rated news program, and we were selling prime commercial air time for a song to low-budget purveyors of hair plugs. . . . You've seen those commercials, right? Well, I analyzed the ratings, and they showed that we were actually holding our own in the first few minutes of the broadcast, but there was a steep drop-off after our hard news coverage wrapped up and we moved on to soft stories—you know, human interest, traffic, weather, sports. Then I analyzed our competitors' broadcasts too, and I noticed that we were giving our audience the same 3 minutes of hard news as all our competitors. So we did some audience testing and found that people actually wanted more hard news, and it was the traffic and accidents that turned them off because they found it depressing. We lengthened our news segment with special investigative reports and condensed our traffic and accident reporting into 30 seconds right before weather and sports. Within 2 months our ratings had shot up from last to first in the time slot, and our advertising revenues had gone up 35 percent. That's the kind of analytical and creative problem solving I could contribute to XYZ Advertising—it's all about examining the audience's needs until you find the market opportunity."

Case in Point: Not on Best Behavior

An interview is a two-way process, so while your interviewers are trying to get a sense of what you'd be like as an employee from your past behavior, you should be scrutinizing their behavior to see what they'd be like as supervisors. If something about your interviewer's behavior strikes you as odd, do your best to overlook it in the interview, but consider it carefully before you accept the job to be sure you can live with it. Consider this extreme case of a bad match:

"Once when I was in my early twenties, I was thrilled because I had made it past the first interview for what I thought was a prime position in my field in New York. Then in the second round, I met with a bigwig in the company. She was perfectly coiffed and put together, but then she started chain smoking neurotically in the interview—and she was seven months pregnant! I was flustered and horrified, and I don't think I was able to completely hide that fact during the interview . . . there were long, awkward silences. I definitely passed judgment on her, and if you don't want to know someone you're just not going to do well in an interview. I'm still embarrassed about it, even though I don't think I would have wanted to work for her—if I saw her on the street I'd cringe.

Hypothetical

Hypothetical questions are the curve balls of the interviewing game. Interviewers throw them at you to test your ability to think on your feet and react using your best professional instincts. A job interview seldom consists only of hypothetical scenarios, since this is not an effective approach to gauge a job candidate's skills or competencies on its own. Hypothetically speaking, anyone might be able to achieve nuclear fission—but few of us could actually demonstrate a potential to make it happen based on past performance (unless you're Albert Einstein). So expect hypothetical questions to pop up occasionally in your interviews, but the bulk of your questions will probably be behavior-based.

What to expect. Hypothetical questions begin with "How would you . . ." or "Imagine if you were to . . ." or "What would you do if . . ." Hypothetical questions are by their very nature hard to anticipate, but don't allow yourself to be blindsided by them. If you need to, use these tricks to buy yourself some thinking time:

- Restate the question: "Let me get this straight: What would I do if . . ."
- Praise the question: "That's a good question. Let me think about that . . ."
- Ask for specifics: "What resources would be available to the team to solve this problem?"

Sample hypothetical questions.

1. If one of your teammates was falling behind on a project you were working on together because of problems at home, how would you handle the situation?

2. How would you deal with an employee whom you suspected of asking for inflated travel expense reimbursements?

3. Imagine you were allowed to institute any new workplace policy you wished for 1 week. What would that be, and why?

Special preparations. Tie the hypothetical problem to a similar or related past experience you've handled well. For example, if you were to be asked the second question above about inflated travel expenses, you might answer as follows:

"I always find that the easiest way to deal with a suspected breach of workplace ethics is to first explain the company policy in a casual, impersonal way, so that there are no misunderstandings about what is expected and no feelings hurt. I once felt that I was being overcharged by a vendor who was sending in invoices that were a little vague on services rendered for dollars spent. I explained to the vendor that while the company didn't necessarily require a time card, the company did need a detailed accounting for time spent by project on every invoice. Lo and behold, the invoices that came in were significantly lower than they had been—and our working relationship was stronger than ever. So I think I might go with a similar approach in this case: Ask everyone on the team to provide annotated receipts with their travel expense report, then check over that employee's receipts—and spot check the rest of the team's, too, just to be fair. I'd also be sure to do the same myself, to set a good example."

Case in Point: Hypothetical vs. Rhetorical Questions

Technically, there should be no such thing as a wrong answer to a hypothetical question. But sometimes employers will turn hypothetical questions into rhetorical questions, hoping you will pick up on their cues and give them the answers they are looking for. If you don't take the hint and give another answer instead, it can be hard to recover. But as career counselor Rosanne Lurie suggests, you can always take the direct approach and ask, "How would you like to have had that resolved?" But there's a certain type of directness that can be counterproductive, as described in this case:

"At one interview, the guy who was doing the hiring asked me, 'Do you love our software product? Do you?' I decided to be honest and say 'Actually, no, I don't.' That sent him around the bend, as they say."

WetFeet®

Case Analysis

This is an interviewing approach most commonly used in the worlds of business consulting, finance, marketing, business operations, and development. Case questions are intended to test a candidate's abilities to analyze a problem or opportunity, perform under pressure, make use of appropriate resources, come up with creative solutions, and communicate and present ideas effectively. Some organizations reserve case questions for the second round of interviews, and even give candidates a chance to prepare responses—but many organizations fire case questions at candidates in the very first round, to weed out as many candidates as possible early on in the interview process.

What to expect. These questions don't sound like questions at all, but more like the story problems you might remember from your GRE or SAT tests. They present a series of facts, variables, and resources, and then ask you to answer a specific question given this data. With case questions, your interviewer may or may not respond to a request for additional details, but you can usually ask your interviewer to repeat the relevant data to make sure you have your facts straight.

There are four common types of case questions:

1. Market-sizing questions ask the candidate to estimate the size of a given market.

2. Business operations cases pose questions about the running of a business.

3. Business strategy questions focus on future business strategy issues, usually with a high-level approach.

4. Resume questions take one of the preceding types and relate it to something from your resume (e.g., career or academic experience), and thus ask you to apply your specialized knowledge.

Sample case questions.

1. **Market sizing:** How many golf carts are there in the United States?

2. **Business operations:** The general manager of a popular ski resort has called on you to help her figure out why her resort has been experiencing declining profits over the past 3 years. How would you help her?

3. **Business strategy:** A French technology outsourcing firm that has done good business with one U.S. microchip-maker now wants to cultivate a broader clientele in Silicon Valley, but they're an outsider in that particular market and are concerned about public perceptions of offshore operations. How would you help them identify market opportunities?

4. **Resume:** I see that you used to work for a major airline. Suppose that your frequent flier program isn't attracting enough new recruits. List options to improve the program while keeping costs down, and then prioritize those ideas according to their relative cost-effectiveness.

Special preparations. Most organizations are careful not to use the same case questions for too long and even vary the questions from one candidate to the next just to ensure that no one has an unfair advantage. That said, advance preparation is essential on case questions, just as it is for any standardized test—familiarity with the common formats, tricks, and logic of case questions will greatly improve your performance. Case questions vary by industry, so you're best off getting some practice with the types of case questions that are most common in your industry. WetFeet's best-selling *Ace Your Case!* series goes into much more detail and provides many practice questions (along with examples of good and bad answers) for those looking down the barrel of the case interview.

Job Simulation

The classic example of the job simulation approach is the typing test. If you can perform the job well in a simulation, you should be able to do it just as well (if not better) in real life. Job simulations are most often used to test candidates in a specific skill area required for the job, such as database QA for a software tester, forklift driving for a warehouse operator, or editing for a proofreader. This may be used in combination with a behavior-based interview or as a screening method to identify the candidates least in need of additional training. It's also a way of finding out whether you're as good as you say you are.

What to expect. If you know your field and have filled a similar position in the recent past, you already know what to expect from a job simulation. Your job simulation may take place on the premises, and you may either be given a strict time limitation or allowed to go at your own pace—but don't take your sweet time, because this may be part of the test! You may be presented with a problem, and challenged with coming back and presenting your solution or findings, such as a graphic designer charged with tweaking a logo. This should be a genuine test of your skills, not a dishonest attempt to get free labor. If you turn in your work, never hear a response, and suddenly see your design on a billboard, you have every right to contact the Better Business Bureau.

Sample questions. There are no standard questions in this type of interview. You'll be expected to walk the talk and show what you can do for the employer. Following are examples of professions and related job simulations:

- Salesperson: Sell me this book.
- Graphic designer: Design a new logo for Bodo's Bagels.
- Teacher: Develop a lesson plan and lead a group of students through that lesson.

Special preparations. You might want to brush up on your technical skills, in case it's been a while since you've put some of them to use. In particular, you should cover any skills you listed on your resume.

Case in Point: Testing Twists

The skills immediately relevant to the job aren't the only abilities that might get put to the test in an interview. Any special skills, talents, or credentials listed on your resume may be put to the test. Consider this story of an unexpected test that left an otherwise confident applicant tongue-tied:

"When I walked into an interview at an online retailer, I was feeling great. I'd done my homework on the organization—I had a firm grasp of its business model, main competitors, the platforms they were using, and the strengths I could bring to the organization to help it capture new business. I'd boned up on case questions, and felt sure I could ace those, too. But who knew that of all the things they could have quizzed me on, it would be the proficiency in Arabic listed on the bottom of my resume that would be put to the test? Turns out the comptroller had been in the Peace Corps in Tunisia, and he conducted the first 10 minutes of the interview in Arabic. I managed to stammer my way through it, even though I hadn't spoken it in ages. Imagine my relief when he switched to English and said, 'I'm glad to see you weren't exaggerating your credentials. So many people do in business these days, and I think it's important to call people out on it.' After I survived that initial trial by fire, the interview was much more relaxed—and I got the job."

Panel Interviews

The one interview approach most likely to make job applicant break out in a cold sweat is the panel interview. Two or more interviewers meet with a candidate at once in this scenario, and after the candidate leaves, the interviewers compare notes and assess the candidate. A panel interview can come at the beginning of the hiring process, right after the initial phone screen or job fair screen, or it may come after the candidate has already been through one or more preliminary one-on-one interviews with an HR representative or manager and/or a job simulation.

What to expect. Many job applicants think of the panel interview as a tense courtroom scenario, where they have to make their case to skeptical judges looking for inconsistencies in the testimony. But a panel interview actually seldom resembles a made-for-TV legal drama—in fact, it's usually more similar to a congenial conversation over lunch, with questions interwoven with discussion of shared concerns and possible solutions. In fact, some panel interviews take place over a perfectly pleasant lunch, rather than in some stuffy boardroom. Interviewers actually tend to be more sensitive about putting the candidate on the spot in panel interviews, so this may work in your favor, too. Even if one interviewer does start to fire tough questions at you, chances are another panel member will empathize with your plight and lob an easier question your way.

Sample questions. The questions in a panel interview are likely to be a combination of behavioral and hypothetical queries. Depending on your industry, this might be when some case questions come up, too. See the sample questions in the preceding sections.

Special preparations. The same preparations described in the previous chapters apply here: Do your background research, know which strengths you plan to emphasize, prepare stories that illustrate these strengths, and have some insightful questions ready to ask your interviewers. The tricky part is making the conversation comfortable among multiple participants, much as you would as a host at a dinner party. If you're not a big fan of dinner parties, you might role-play a panel interview with some friends to get more comfortable with the idea. That way, if you get tense in the actual interview, you can imagine you are just talking with your friends again to help you relax. In the interview, put on your best dinner-party-host manners and make sure that you share your attention around to all the panelists. Make eye contact with each person, and greet and shake hands with each one if possible. If you miss someone's name when the introductions are being made, don't be afraid to interject and ask for it to be repeated so that you can call each person by name. When the questions begin, you can direct your attention primarily to the individual who posed the question, but be sure to look around and engage others so that it doesn't become an exclusive two-way conversation. If one interviewer is firing questions at you or otherwise dominating the conversation, redirect your attention to pull in the others.

Physical Screenings: Know Your Rights

Drug screenings and fitness tests are part of the selection process in a wide number of industries, so you shouldn't be surprised if these are part of the process for an interview. Some companies make job offers contingent upon a clean drug-test result, and positions that require physical exertion can also request you to take a fitness test before offering you the job. However, it is illegal for employers to require you to take any psychological tests or medical examinations before you're offered a position. You should be aware that as a condition of proceeding to the next stage of the hiring process, you might be asked to take a drug screening test. Even if you're an adept pilot, an airline won't want to entrust you with hundreds of passengers if you are often under the influence of controlled substances. You can refuse to take the test, of course, but the employer can also refuse to hire you.

Concluding Gracefully

- Ask Really Good Questions
- Have an Exit Strategy
- Follow Up

You've made a stellar first impression—congratulations! Now is your chance to cinch the deal by leaving your interviewer with a positive final impression. Before you walk out that door, be sure you've asked a few good questions, executed an effective exit strategy, and are ready and willing to follow through with a postinterview recap and a timely, thoughtful thank-you note. If you do, you may soon be coming back through that office door for a second interview or to report for work at your new job.

Ask Really Good Questions

Many candidates focus on answering hard questions in an interview, but the most promising candidates come prepared to ask them, too. If you don't ask questions, your interviewer may take it as a sign that you either "are not that interested in the job, or just aren't prepared," says Rosanne Lurie, licensed career counselor. "That leaves your interviewer thinking, 'If you can't be bothered to come up with a few questions, why should I bother with you?'" This is not the impression you want to leave with your interviewer—so be sure to have some questions ready to ask at the end of the interview, if they haven't come up already in the course of the interview.

How do you know what's a good question to ask? You should have some idea from your background research what kinds of questions would be appropriate to ask about the position and the organization to determine whether they're a good fit for you and your career plans. But ideally, your question should not just help you suss out the position—it should help you land it. A good question does this in three ways:

1. **It reveals your knowledge of the industry and/or company.** The time you spent reading news stories, trade publications, and annual reports enables you to ask a well-informed question like, "I know you recently merged with Company X, and mergers often place demands on the communications department on multiple fronts—developing a new corporate identity, bridging two corporate cultures, fielding media requests. What do you see as the greatest burden on the communications team as a result of the merger, and how do you think I could be of the greatest help to the team in this area?"

2. **It shows that you've been paying close attention to your interviewer.** It's fine if a few of your questions are a little generic—odds are, your interviewer asked you some generic questions, too. But if you take a few notes during the interview, you can refer to comments your interviewer made to personalize your questions. Instead of asking, "What personal attributes do you think will be most helpful in this position?" use your notes to tailor your question as follows: "You mentioned that excelling in this position takes perseverance and grace under pressure. What other personal attributes do you think would be especially useful in this job?"

3. **It establishes a personal connection.** If you spend the entire interview talking about yourself and the job, it won't be the kind of bonding experience that would stand out in an interviewer's mind. Besides, most people like to talk about themselves—so provide an opening for your interviewer to reveal personal insights by asking, "How did you start working with this organization? What keeps you here and interested in your job?"

Ten Very Good Questions to Ask and 1 Essential Question

1. What three words would you use to describe the work environment here?
2. What would you say are the organization's greatest opportunities in the next 3 years?
3. What would you say are the organization's greatest challenges in the next 3 years?
4. How has [major business trend or current event] affected your organization?
5. What are the greatest learning opportunities you've had at [name of organization]?
6. What do you like most about working here?
7. What do you find most challenging about working here?
8. Can you describe three specific opportunities for growth this position offers?
9. What do you see as the potential drawbacks of this position?
10. What personal qualities do the teammates you value most possess?

... and the most important question of all:

What are the next steps I should take to be hired for this position?

Touchy Subjects

Questions about turnover, expected working hours, and stress levels can be difficult to broach, but if you can ask them sensitively you'll find out whether this is a place you really want to work—and show that you know your worth and want to be part of an organization that values its employees. "Timing is important for these delicate questions," notes Rosanne Lurie. "Wait to pose them until later in the interview if you're feeling confident, or hold off until a second or third interview." When you do broach the subject, says Lurie, make sure your tone is casual and conversational: "There should be no anxiety or confrontational make-or-break tone to your question." Instead of asking a direct and potentially awkward question about why the last person left the position, Lurie advises, "ask what changes came about that created this position." If you've developed rapport with your interviewer, you can ask personal questions like, "Is this a good place to work? What is it like here?"

Case in Point: Turnabout Is Fair Play

If you're less impressed with a job the more you hear about it, you might want to probe the positives and negatives of the position rather than focusing on selling yourself for a position you might not want. Consider the following case of an awkward interview and even more awkward job offer:

"After I sweated through a very difficult interview at a religiously affiliated organization, during which I was grilled about my qualifications and asked uncomfortable [not to mention illegal] questions about my religious beliefs and marital status, my interviewer finally invited me to ask a few questions. By this point, I had a hunch that this might not be the easiest place to work and was willing to bet the last person had left due to stress, so I delicately asked how the position became available. Bingo! The interviewer admitted the last person left due to a nervous breakdown. So I wrapped up the interview politely yet swiftly. I only wished I'd spared us both the trouble by asking the question earlier in the interview! By then I'd sold them on my strong points and they actually offered me the job, so I had to backpedal and explain that it sounded like the work environment was more stressful than seemed healthy."

Have an Exit Strategy

Once you've asked at least two or three questions and received answers, you'll know the interview is coming to a close. Don't wait until your interviewer is out of steam and all talked out to start wrapping things up—it's always better to leave a potential employer wanting more! When you sense the energy level is beginning to dip and before your interviewer cuts the interview off abruptly, start putting your exit strategy into action.

A sound exit strategy consists of seven steps:

1. Make Amends

Now is your final chance to modify any answers you don't think you answered particularly well, or clarify your reasoning behind an answer that didn't seem to please your interviewer. As long as you can leave them satisfied that your reasoning is sound, interviewers won't be so concerned they didn't get an answer they were after. "I don't want to take too much more of your time, but I did want to get back to that question you asked me about how I'd handle a tough customer. Just to clarify, I wouldn't recommend referring the customer to a supervisor until I'd made every offer I am authorized to make to put things right."

2. Make Your Final Pitch

Remind your interviewer of the three main reasons why you are a good match for this position in a minute or less. Think of it this way: Your interviewer is your target buyer, and your strengths are the very special package deal you're selling. According to the time-honored marketing Law of Seven, the average consumer doesn't hear a sales message until it's been stated seven times—so don't be shy about repeating your strengths one last time. Make your final sales message clear, quick, and memorable, and you just might cinch the deal.

3. Say You Want the Job

Don't leave any doubt in your interviewer's mind about your interest in the position. Sometimes interviewers won't offer the job to well-qualified candidates they fear are disinterested, overqualified, or otherwise might be "settling" for a job they don't really want. Interviewers dread rejection too—no one wants to get their heart set on a candidate who then turns down the job. So if you let your interviewer know you want the job, you've removed one more possible obstacle to a job offer. Look your interviewer right in the eye and say, "I was excited about this position even before I came in today, but after talking to you I'm more certain than ever that I really want this job." But be sure you mean it, because there's always a chance your interviewer may respond, "Great. When can you start?"

4. Ask About Next Steps

If the interviewer doesn't give you a definite answer right away and says they'll let you know, don't be disappointed or dissuaded. This isn't necessarily an easy let-down; they may just need to check in with colleagues to schedule a second (or third) interview or confirm an offer. Ask how soon you should follow up, and mention that you'd be delighted to have the chance to meet the rest of the team.

5. Ask Whether They Have Any Other Questions for You

This gives you a chance to address any issues that might be left unresolved in your interviewers' minds and shows that you are attuned to their concerns. If your interviewers say, "No, that about covers it," you should take the hint and thank them for their time.

6. Give Your Interviewer Something to Remember You by

A business card would be ideal, and an article by or about you would be an impressive bonus. At the very least, hand your interviewer an extra copy of your resume—everything you can do to keep your candidacy top of mind and top of inbox helps.

7. Make a Smooth Move for the Door

Look your interviewer in the eye and offer a few words of appreciation for how much you got out of your conversation. Here's an example: "I have to thank you again for taking time to meet with me today. You really got me thinking about the potential for growth in this industry and this organization, and I would welcome the opportunity this position offers to contribute to that growth." Then be sure you have all your belongings and offer your interviewer a warm handshake and smile. This is a powerful last impression to leave with your interviewer: personal, meaningful, and consummately professional. This handshake should mark the end of your interview, and the beginning of a rewarding professional relationship.

Case in Point: Closing Remarks Close the Deal

When you make your final comments to your interviewer, remember that you have nothing to lose and everything to gain. Consider this last-minute success story:

"When I was 24, I interviewed for a job at a weekly newspaper in Budapest. The publisher and executive editor were jowly 40- and 50-something Brits with gray suits, who appeared to be interviewing me as a courtesy to the friend who'd recommended me. They asked a few rather standard questions and didn't particularly seem to be listening to the answers; I was sure that I didn't have the job. So I had nothing to lose. After I was done answering their questions, I said, 'Look, I'm a damn good editor and a damn good writer, and both are in short supply. And I know you'd prefer someone a bit older, with more connections locally—but I'm good, and I'm smart, and I'm willing to work awfully hard. So I think you should hire me.' They sort of stammered and were taken aback, and I very sweetly closed things up—told them to call if they had any other questions, and said that I'd check back in a week or so to follow up. I got a call 2 days later. And a job offer."

Follow Up

Once the interview is over, you should review your notes from the interview and start planning your follow-up. If your interviewer told you to follow up in a week, mark that date in your calendar and be sure to call then for a "status check" and reiterate your willingness to meet with other members of the team. (Just remember, there's a fine line between talking and stalking—if you've called two or three times over the course of a couple of weeks and there's still no definitive response one way or another, you may want to downshift your follow-up contacts to e-mail at less frequent intervals.) Take a minute to review your performance, and identify areas where you excelled and areas you might improve upon in future interviews. Your notes can also help you identify experiences you neglected to mention or questions you'd like to ask in follow-up interviews.

Thank-You Notes

While the interview is still fresh in your mind, sit down with any notes you took during the interview and craft a warm, personal thank-you message. Much has been written on the importance of prompt, personal thank-you notes—but although virtually every career advisor emphasizes how important they are, many candidates overlook this perfectly sound professional advice. Put other candidates' oversight to your advantage, and send thanks no later than the day after your interview. A typed note on business stationary or a legible, handwritten note on an elegant card (no gag cards) would be ideal, but don't spend ages looking for the perfect card or wordsmithing your note to death. A quick, sincere e-mail is preferable to a stunning card that arrives 10 days after your interview, when the interviewer has already forgotten your name and offered the job to someone else.

In addition to showing your appreciation for your interviewer's time, a thank you note is a prime opportunity to:

- Mention something you neglected in your resume.
- Alleviate any concerns raised in the interview.
- Convey your enthusiasm.
- Reiterate key strengths you possess that relate to the job.

Here's how a thank-you note might read:

Sample Thank-You Letter

Dear Ms. Gonzales,

Thank you again for a most inspiring meeting. I know how hectic a head chef's schedule can get right before a restaurant opening and how many resumes you must have received for the assistant chef position, so I am especially appreciative of your taking the time to meet with me and share your insights on the business. I picked up a copy of that issue of *Gourmet* you mentioned, and you're so right—that feature article on Tuscany really missed the boat! There's so much more to Tuscan cuisine than steak and white beans, as you've demonstrated in your cookbook. I look forward to branching out from Neapolitan cuisine, and am sure our regional specializations will prove a fitting complement for one another—and a delicious one, at that.

I look forward to continuing our conversation in the kitchen at LouLou in the near future.

Best regards,

Sally

p.s. Your friend and mine, Ruthie, sends her best, and says to say thanks for the pork chop tips.

Case in Point: The Power of Thanks

A few words of appreciation can go a long way to building your professional reputation and your career. Consider this story of a particularly resilient and appreciative job-seeker:

"When we were hiring for a support position, we interviewed a guy who turned out to be far too qualified for the position. We got such a nice note from him, we felt obliged to call and tell him he didn't get the job—even though our usual modus operandi is just to not call the interviewee back. Far from being crushed, he actually wrote us another note thanking us for taking the time to let him know, and mentioned that he would keep an eye out for future opportunities with the company.

"True to his word, he applied again 6 months later for a position in the editorial department. We actually offered it to a candidate with more editorial experience, who turned it down. So we decided to take a chance on an enthusiastic candidate who was willing to learn, and there was a file with this guy's resume and follow-up notes floating around the office. . . . I don't know if it was divine intervention or the sheer power of suggestion, but he got the job."

For Your Reference

- Additional Interviewing Resources
- General Interviewing Advice
- Job Search Resources
- Background Research Tools
- Salary Negotiation Tools

Additional Interviewing Resources

With a little extra research, you can prepare for some of the less obvious questions interviewers will ask. Rather than inventing these questions themselves, interviewers often pull them from professional resources you, too, can access: the Internet, human resource and development services, interview books, and workplace advice columnists. Here's how to find them:

Internet Searches

Run a Google search on "interview questions" or "job interview questions" and check out the search results to find the most popular (top 20) websites that list interview questions employers should ask. Chances are, interviewers who are pressed for time will be on the same (Web) page as you when it comes time to prepare for their end of the interview—so make a note of any questions you find on more than one website, and prepare your responses to those key questions. Sites such as www.job-interview.net offer lists of some of the toughest interview questions and appropriate responses, too.

HR and Recruitment Services

Spend a while thinking like a recruiter or HR professional, and you'll be better prepared for their questions. HR professionals make an effort to stay on the cutting edge of interview best practices, so boning up on current interviewing trends will help you anticipate questions you might face before an HR representative or recruiter. Look up HR professional associations and HR and recruiter professional websites and run a keyword search on "interviewing," and see if you can find recommended questions or practices. Sites such as HR Internet Guide (www.hr-guide.com) offer valuable lists of interview questions and outline other ways HR professionals test candidate competencies. Your background research should have helped you identify the competencies interviewers will be looking for in candidates for a position

Books

If you are looking for work in a field that follows a specialized interview process, look for books that specifically address that interview type. WetFeet publishes the four-volume Ace Your Case! series of Insider Guides for consulting interviews, which rely heavily on the dreaded case question. For those looking to work in the investment banking industry, check out *Beat the Street: The WetFeet Insider Guide to Investment Banking Interviews.*

General Interviewing Advice

For a leg up on the competition, peruse these general interviewing advice sources:

WetFeet's Interviewing Advice

www.wetfeet.com/advice/interviewing.asp

Covers every interviewing scenario from brainteasing case quizzes to deceptively casual lunch meetings, and offers tips for dealing with tricky situations such as getting unflattering references, arriving late for an interview, and turning down a job offer.

Job-Interview.net

www.job-interview.net

Insights from top career counselors, a database of 900 common interview questions and samples of excellent answers, tips to perfect your skills with mock interviews, and much more.

National Association of Colleges and Employers' Career Library

www.jobweb.com/Resources

In-depth information on job fairs, thank-you notes, and other interview concerns, plus salary and job outlook data, job fair listings, college career center resources, and features on employers.

MSN's Interviewing Advice

msn.careerbuilder.com/Custom/MSN/CareerAdvice/Interviewing.htm

Helpful hints on interview fashion blunders, calming your jitters, putting a positive spin on your role at a now-defunct company, and other interview issues.

HR Guide to Legal Issues

www.hr-guide.com/data/075.htm

If you feel an employer has asked you inappropriate interview questions, use this site to review the legalities of interviewing and learn more about your recourse under the law.

Job Search Resources

Books

Networking Works! The WetFeet Insider Guide to Networking

Many job vacancies are filled before an opening is announced publicly—but follow these strategies for effective networking, and you'll tap into this hidden job market.

Get Your Foot in the Door! The WetFeet Insider Guide to Landing the Job Interview

Don't just send out resumes and hope for the best—let this guide show you how to use cover letters, phone calls, and e-mail to get your foot in the door.

Job Hunting A to Z: The WetFeet Insider Guide to Landing the Job You Want

This information-packed guide covers networking, interviewing, and negotiation all in one handy reference, with tips on drumming up contacts and referrals, handling weird interview situations, and choosing from several offers.

Websites

American Staffing Association

www.staffingtoday.net

The "Selecting a Firm" tips on this site can help you find a staffing company that will seek out jobs for you and advocate on your behalf in the job market.

Employment Law Information Network

www.elinfonet.com

Concerned that visa status, fitness, or drug testing requirements might be barriers in your job search? Get the latest on legal hiring requirements on the "Hot Topics" section of this site.

Background Research Tools

WetFeet's Company Profiles and Interviews

www.wetfeet.com/research/companies.asp

Get the lowdown on hundreds of high-profile employers, including key numbers, personnel highlights, key facts, and an overview for each company. A free service provided by WetFeet.

***Fortune* Career Resources**

www.fortune.com/fortune/careers

Fortune's annual reports on the best places to work, most admired companies, and the best places to work for women and minorities are key background reading. Also check out their columns to discover jobs you never new existed ("You Do What?"), the latest on workplace practices such as telecommuting and casual dress, and career quizzes.

Bureau of Labor Statistics

www.bls.gov/oco/home.htm

Search the Career Guide to Industries and the Occupational Outlook Handbook to research opportunities in your field and explore the most promising career options. The Occupational Employment Statistics will help you identify mean salaries, the current rate of layoffs, and wage comparisons for your industry and geographic location. Check out the Occupational Outlook Quarterly's special report, "Employment Interviewing: Seizing the Opportunity and the Job," at www.bls.gov/opub/ooq/2000/summer/art02.htm.

Business Week Company Research

http://bwnt.businessweek.com:/company/search.asp

Get the inside scoop on some 4,000 employers. While you're there, check out *Business Week's* "Career Strategies" section for job search strategies for MBAs, downsized midcareer employees, and aspiring executives.

U.S. Census Bureau

www.census.gov

Check out the latest economic census figures as of March 2004, including earnings for your industry, earnings cross-referenced by occupation, education level and gender for your geographic location, and hard numbers on e-commerce.

Labor Market Information Center

www.careeronestop.org/lmi/LMIHome.asp

Find out what occupations are hottest in your geographic area and across the nation.

Current Economic Conditions by Federal Reserve District

www.federalreserve.gov/FOMC/BeigeBook/2004/

If you're considering relocating to look for work, use this government index known as the "Beige Book" to identify where the economic prospects are brightest in the United States.

The Conference Board

www.conference-board.org

Concerned about what those economic indicators mean for your industry—and your job prospects? Get expert perspective on business trends using the Conference Board's research in articles such as "Will We All Be Unemployed?" and "Escape from Corporate America: The New Women Entrepreneurs."

Salary Negotiation Tools

The WetFeet Insider Guide to Negotiating Your Salary and Perks

Get your way without breaking the deal or even a sweat with WetFeet's comprehensive guide to the niceties of negotiation. Covers bargaining power, salary histories, extra perks, and evaluating offers.

America's Career InfoNet

www.acinet.org

Find median wages for your chosen field in your geographic location, what it takes for you to get ahead in your occupation, and which careers have the strongest outlook right now.

Salary.com

www.salary.com

Find appropriate salary and benefits for your position and pick up tips on how to raise your pay, get paid time off, and negotiate cost-of-living increases.

Professional Association for Compensation, Benefits, and Total Rewards

www.worldatwork.org/

Check out the latest research on performance-based pay, stock options, overtime pay, and paid leave though survey briefs and in-depth reports.

WetFeet's Insider Guide Series

Ace Your Case! The WetFeet Insider Guide to Consulting Interviews
Ace Your Case II: Fifteen More Consulting Cases
Ace Your Case III: Practice Makes Perfect
Ace Your Case IV: The Latest and Greatest
Ace Your Interview! The WetFeet Insider Guide to Interviewing
Beat the Street: The WetFeet Insider Guide to Investment Banking Interviews
Getting Your Ideal Internship
Get Your Foot in the Door! Landing the Job Interview
Job Hunting A to Z: The WetFeet Insider Guide to Landing the Job You Want
Killer Consulting Resumes!
Killer Cover Letters and Resumes!
Killer Investment Banking Resumes!
Negotiating Your Salary and Perks
Networking Works! The WetFeet Insider Guide to Networking

Career and Industry Guides

Accounting
Advertising and Public Relations
Asset Management and Retail Brokerage
Biotech and Pharmaceuticals
Brand Management
Health Care
Human Resources
Computer Software and Hardware
Consulting for Ph.D.s, Lawyers, and Doctors
Industries and Careers for MBAs
Industries and Careers for Undergrads
Information Technology
Investment Banking

Management Consulting
Manufacturing
Marketing and Market Research
Non-Profits and Government Agencies
Oil and Gas
Real Estate
Sports and Entertainment
Supply Chain Management
Top 20 Biotechnology and Pharmaceutical Firms
Top 25 Consulting Firms
Top 25 Financial Services Firms
Top 20 Law Firms
Venture Capital

Company Guides

Accenture
Bain & Company
Bear Stearns
Booz Allen Hamilton
The Boston Consulting Group
Cap Gemini Ernst & Young
Citigroup's Corporate and Investment Bank
Credit Suisse First Boston
Deloitte Consulting
Goldman Sachs
IBM Business Consulting Services
JPMorgan Chase
Lehman Brothers
McKinsey & Company
Merrill Lynch
Monitor Group
Morgan Stanley